From Dreamtime to Armageddon

Phillip Gray

BALBOA
PRESS
A DIVISION OF HAY HOUSE

Copyright © 2018 Phillip Gray.

Interior Graphics/Art Credit: Roland Schicht and Richard Clark

All rights reserved. No part of this book may be used or reproduced by any means, graphic, electronic, or mechanical, including photocopying, recording, taping or by any information storage retrieval system without the written permission of the author except in the case of brief quotations embodied in critical articles and reviews.

Balboa Press books may be ordered through booksellers or by contacting:

Balboa Press
A Division of Hay House
1663 Liberty Drive
Bloomington, IN 47403
www.balboapress.com.au
1 (877) 407-4847

Because of the dynamic nature of the Internet, any web addresses or links contained in this book may have changed since publication and may no longer be valid. The views expressed in this work are solely those of the author and do not necessarily reflect the views of the publisher, and the publisher hereby disclaims any responsibility for them.

The author of this book does not dispense medical advice or prescribe the use of any technique as a form of treatment for physical, emotional, or medical problems without the advice of a physician, either directly or indirectly. The intent of the author is only to offer information of a general nature to help you in your quest for emotional and spiritual well-being. In the event you use any of the information in this book for yourself, which is your constitutional right, the author and the publisher assume no responsibility for your actions.

Any people depicted in stock imagery provided by Getty Images are models, and such images are being used for illustrative purposes only.
Certain stock imagery © Getty Images.

Print information available on the last page.

ISBN: 978-1-5043-1373-5 (sc)
ISBN: 978-1-5043-1374-2 (e)

Balboa Press rev. date: 07/09/2018

*Some of this story is fiction. Some of it is fact.
I will leave it up to the reader to
determine which is which.*

I would like to express my unreserved thanks to Uncle David Tournier (now deceased)... the past Indigenous Cultural Language Co-Ordinator and Education Officer, as well as to Trevor James (Reg) Abrahams... the Cultural Heritage Officer of the WATHAURONG ABORIGINAL CO-OPERATIVE LTD, both of whom gave me their support and their permission to use certain information in this book pertaining to the Wathaurong culture.

Signed, the Author.

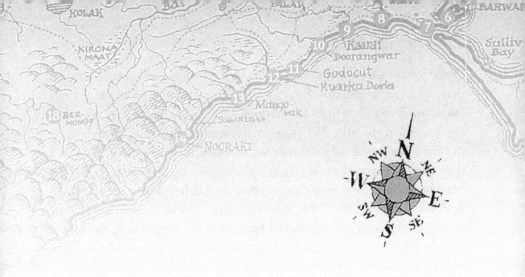

INTRODUCTION

Although fifteen years had passed since the First Fleet's arrival at Botany Bay, the French were still showing more than a passing interest in that vast southern continent in *spite* of the British presence there. So with further expansion of the fledgling colony now becoming a pressing priority, the British powers-that-be based in Sydney commissioned Acting Lieutenant John Murray to explore the country's southern coastline to try to find a suitable location to help bolster Britain's position. As a result, Murray set out from Sydney in the *'Lady Nelson'* in November 1801 with a crew of fifteen, before going on to discover what would eventually become known as Port Phillip Bay, where he raised the Union Jack high upon a bluff at the site of present-day Sorrento.

Meanwhile, back home in England where another shipment of convicts was being prepared for dispatch to New South Wales, word arrived of the forests of valuable timber said to be growing in abundance around the shores of this new location, and after a hasty meeting of those in authority, it was decided that a *second* convict colony should be established there.

With Colonel David Collins appointed to the role of Lieutenant Governor, those mustered together to form the new colony were to make the journey out from England in two British vessels: The first ship *"Calcutta"* was commissioned to carry 307 convicts (including some of their wives and children) along with 50 royal marines and Governor Collins with his civil staff, while the second vessel *"Ocean"* would carry a few free settlers and the settlement stores. However, after dropping anchor in a sheltered Port Phillip Bay cove in October 1803, it soon became apparent that the soil was too poor to farm and that the region lacked fresh water, so not wishing to prolong what he quickly came to regard as a sorry mistake, Collins wasted no time in seeking permission to relocate the settlement to Van Diemen's Land. Approval was granted a short time later and the move got under way.

Although the Sullivan Bay settlement lasted little more than a few short months, during that time a number of convicts managed to escape into the bush.

One of these men was William Buckley:

Born in Cheshire England in 1780 and raised by his maternal grandparents in nearby Macclesfield … as soon as he was old enough to make his own way in the world, Buckley served an apprenticeship in the bricklaying trade, before leaving home at the age of nineteen to enlist in the service of the King's Guard.

Becoming a formidable presence as he grew into manhood, he towered over his fellow soldiers at a lofty 6 feet 8 inches when the average height of British men in uniform was a mere 5 feet 6. However, it has long been said that the bigger they are the harder they fall, and after being wounded in action while fighting for his country in the Napoleonic wars, Buckley was repatriated back home to his native England. There is also a saying that idle hands are the devil's workshop, and without the discipline of the King's Guard to help keep him in line - along with the volatile combination of strong ale and loose women thrown into the mix - one sad and sorry night whilst trying to impress a lady to whom he had taken a fancy, Buckley and one of his friends were caught stealing two bolts of cloth in an act of drunken bravado, and were sentenced to transportation for the rest of their lives.

The following story is what happened next:

CHAPTER 1
13TH OCTOBER 1803

Here I stand ... a whole world away from the place I call home, and though the sight of these tree-lined shores seem pleasant enough to the eye, they are not the cliffs of Dover. Having finally dropped anchor after many long months at sea, we are lying a quarter mile offshore alongside our sister ship, while I gaze at a shoreline of golden sand and upon hills of rolling green. As I was given the role of man-servant to the governor on the journey out from England, I am the only prisoner fortunate enough to be not currently locked below, while all other able-bodied men have been put to work unloading the ships until it is deemed safe to take the rest of us unwilling guests of His Majesty ashore. As I pause to reflect upon those past few months at sea - when I compare it to the months that I had previously spent in the disease-ridden hulk of the *Portland* (where many of the prisoners were dropping like flies) my journey down to this southern land has been more like a picnic. As far as my role as man-servant was concerned, I will let you in on a little secret - I was often given the liberty of assisting the crew with their chores up on deck whenever our commander had seen fit to entertain a certain lady (the wife of one of our fellow-prisoners) alone in his cabin.

And now that the governor has gone ashore to oversee the landing, I have been able to linger here alone and unattended, smelling the warm sea air and watching those on the beach busying themselves like ants upon a crust of bread. But please do not judge me as one unsympathetic to those poor wretched souls below, for I have shared their chains of iron and have also felt the lash, it's just that on *this* occasion I am the lucky one and have slipped through the net.

For the second day in a row I've seen them ferrying the stores to the beach. I saw them lower the wagons … the cattle, the goats and the pigs, while I watched their tents of calico popping up along the sea strand like new-season's mushrooms in autumn.

So now I stand and I wait and I wonder and I watch as wisps of smoke billow and curl from the campfires lining the shore. I breathe a sigh as my lazy gaze follows the grey-green line of the land rolling mile upon mile for as far as the eye can see. But alas not for me the fields of England, not for me the hills of old. The whole morning long I've been hearing the axes' bite from yonder across bay. Heard the cannon roar up there on the bluff, and the drum for the start of day. Now it is a party of marines that catches my eye in their coats of blazing red, and as I watch them enter the longboat and steer toward where I stand, I take off my hat and I turn on my heels … it is high time I went below.

A week has passed since we came ashore, and the settlement grows bigger by the day, nestled here as it is in this sheltered cove on a 400 yard ribbon of sand. Rumour has it that the parties sent out to explore for water have returned with nothing to report but disappointment, and that if it pleases the Almighty we will all be called upon to drink the salty brine from the wooden casks which they have sunk in the sand to filter the seawater. And I can assure you of one thing beyond any doubt … I will not be the only one praying for rain.

Positioned out here as we are upon this ancient sea strand, the encampment lies between one sandstone bluff pointing out to sea at the eastern end of the beach, while another one just like it guards the west. Off to the south are the wilds of the bush, and beyond that … who knows what? The aforementioned western bluff is where they have put up the hospital tent, while to the rear of that are the convict tents. And whilst on the subject of those convict tents, let me remind you that each and every one of those tents is a sad and silent keeper of a whole world of secrets. See over yonder the marines' tents? It goes without saying but I will say it nonetheless ... those rogues are little more than an odd assortment of scoundrels brought here to guard us so-called dregs of the earth. Or to put it in the more eloquent words of Mister Collins: *"They who have been selected by their sovereign to compose the Garrison for the protection of this infant colony."* They call the clearing over yonder the parade ground, though it is little more than a patch of sand. But far be it for the likes of me to offer views on military affairs ... opinions are little more than leaves before the wind when a man is not free to be heard.

Further along the shore are the storage tents, each one being guarded around the clock. The foundations for the munitions battery are beginning to take shape too, and please forgive my bragging, but my skills in the trade of bricks and mortar have been called upon to help with its construction. See those two big cooking caldrons simmering over a fire? One is being used as the military laundry.

And while on the subject of that laundry, allow me to quote Mister Collins again: *"The Commanding Officer directs and appoints the following women to be employed in the following manner... the wife of Private William Bean to wash for 15 persons. The wife of Private George Curley to wash for 15 persons, and the wife of Private James Spooner to wash for 14 persons."* The enclosures off to the left are for the livestock - the cattle, the sheep and the pigs, while those yonder coops are for the housing of Reverend Knopwood's hens. As we approach the eastern headland, we come to the settlers' tents positioned close by to the officer's tents. And if we raise our gaze to the top of that eastern headland, we will see the largest tent of all ... for the housing of Mister Collins. And there at the crest of that rocky outcrop, sharing the bluff with that grand marquee stand two bold cannons pointing out to the sea while the Union Jack flutters in the breeze.

So that is the long and the short of this God-forsaken settlement ... some four hundred souls all cast ashore, here at the end of the earth.

Five weeks have passed since our arrival, with each day getting hotter than the last, while I wait and I watch and I listen and I toil and I dream my dreams of freedom till the sun comes up. Two more men fled into the bush today, and the marines are out in force trying to track them down. Although I am not the only one of the opinion that those half-witted redcoats could not so much as track an elephant through the snow, let alone two desperate men in an alien bush.

And speaking of that alien bush ... I and three other felons have been out quarrying sandstone, and the aforementioned munitions battery continues to grow as a result. Many rutted tracks run through the encampment now too, as the timber-cutters' wagons roll to and from the mountain. They refer to that mountain as Arthur's Seat, as Mister Collins told me on the day that we arrived:

"Do you see that hill through yonder cloud Mister Buckley? It is called 'Arthur's Seat'. Named thus by John Murray - the first British citizen to sail into this bay, for it reminded him of a hill just like it back home in his native Edinburgh."

Like we that are made to quarry the stone, the timber-cutters *also* have to toil out here till the sun goes down, but the bush gives a taste of freedom not found within four walls. And though we labour quite a distance away from the camp, we still manage to keep abreast of the news. Word will always find an ear, an ear that wants to listen, even in a place like this. And the word passing among the men is that Mister Collins wants to pack up the settlement and move it elsewhere. My own two eyes were given confirmation of this when I watched the boat leave for Sydney little more than two weeks ago. And it is a very long way to travel unless for a matter of great importance. The same word going around says that the boat was carrying a letter for the eyes of the Governor and *his* eyes only. *My* thoughts are that Mister Collins wants to move us all down to Van Diemen's Land, for I heard him speak of that place on the journey out, and I saw the fond look in his eyes.

It pains me to have to tell of three more absconders brought back in chains today, and how we were all mustered around the parade ground ... guards and felons alike, to watch the battle-hardened drummer swing the lash. I am not ashamed to admit that what those three men were made to endure one hundred times over, very nearly brought me to my knees. For to hear a man scream for mercy is not a thing you want to hear, and the smell of flesh hanging off a man's bare back will linger ever-present in my mind. Those poor souls were not the first to try and more are bound to try again, for I have heard men talk of China waiting there across the range, or Sydney town – that's even closer still. But I for one will sit and wait, my time will come I'm sure, death waits for those who flee when unprepared, but we who talk in whispers, we will know when it is time, and there'll be no man shirking it you wait and see.

We have not seen rain in weeks, and I have my suspicions that the brackish water we are being given to drink is the reason why the hospital tent is overflowing with the sick and the infirmed.

Even the marines are far from happy, compelled as they are to chase absconders through the bush, then to march out on parade two times a day. At least the redcoats get their daily half pint of spirits though, which is a half a pint more than the likes of us. Fear of the natives is ever-present too, with stories of skirmishes up on the mount and of blood spilled out in the bush.

As I suspected, news has arrived that the settlement is to be moved to Van Diemen's Land, and the task of building a wharf to load the ships is already getting underway. But of one thing I am certain and I will share it with you now ...

I will not be on that ship, you wait and see.

December 25th beckons, with talk of the move and of Christmas, and thoughts of families back home across the sea. But I will leave such thoughts of England to other souls I say, no Christmas cheer this year will be for me. The chance to flee to Sydney town, catch a ship that's bound for home, that's the sort of dream in such as we.

A man can keep no secrets when under lock and key. He cannot even break wind without half of the convict world listening in to adjudge its merit, and although it was with my old friend **Bill Marmon** that I first began to plan our escape ... our plans had become the plans of *six* before we knew it. Bill and I go way back to those happier days in England, and please allow me take time out to explain: Following my return to England after seeing active service, Bill and I had been enjoying an ale or two in the Lincoln Tavern one cold wintery night when by chance a sweet lady fair just happened to saunter in from the cold. I am no oil painting, plain and simple, but my heart skipped a beat when her eyes met mine and I fell head-over-heels most sure and true. Although I can no longer recollect all of the events that occurred on that fateful night, what I *do* recall is having felt more than a little emboldened by the effects of strong liquor, and as would come to be revealed under later interrogation … Bill and I had undertaken to break and enter the premises of the local tailor, and make a gift to the lady of two handsome rolls of Irish cloth. Needless to say, when the deed was done and the good lady was all smiles and gratitude, the unexpected arrival of the local constabulary came to spoil the party, and the rest as they say, is history.

Bill and I were sent to the hulks at Langstone Harbour and we are now two years older but a whole lot wiser. But wiser or not, we are prisoners nonetheless … down here at Sullivan Bay. As for the rest of our motley group, some of them go back to those earlier days at Langstone: **Tom Page** for example … he was sentenced to death for the charge of highway robbery but like Bill and myself, had his sentence reprieved and has so far lived to tell the tale. Two less serious offenders are **George Pye** and **Charlie Shore.** Charlie was double-chained for insolence on the journey out and carries the scars to prove it. The last of our group is **Dan Mcallenan.** Though there is not much of him at a mere 5ft 4inches, what he lacks in size he more than makes up for with more than his share of rat cunning, and he is Irish through and through. Dan has been able to procure a Brown Bess musket and conceal it at the quarry, a tinder-box he has hidden there as well. The other items we'll be needing I will talk of soon enough. But for now, that is our group in a nutshell … six miserable wretches sent down by the courts to rot upon this antipodean shore, and all of us far from home.

The word doing the rounds is that the guards are to be given a double ration of grog, starting from tomorrow up until the New Year, and judging by the manner in which they handle their *current* allocation, I doubt they'll be able to tell their arse from their elbow by the time that extra liquor starts to flow. Please allow me to give an example of what I mean … although a hungry cat will be alert to its prey, on Christmas Eve, while the guard slept soundly with a belly full of ale, Dan was able to slip right under his nose into the supply tent, and a short time later, he concealed two bags of supplies in the trunk of a hollow tree.

So now we await tomorrow night, with plans to make our break in the camp dinghy, before rowing back to shore at a predetermined point just a few short miles down the coast. From there we intend to divest ourselves of the boat before trekking to the quarry for the musket. And with half an ounce of luck and the Good Lord's grace, by the time they discover we have gone overland, we hope to be miles in the clear and well on our way to Sydney town.

When the sun broke through on Christmas day we were primed and ready to go, biding our time as we awaited the coming of darkness. And while we did so, each and every one of us had sworn an oath: *'Whatever happens … there will be no turning back.'*

By 9:00 pm there was neither moon nor stars to light the way, and while a thunderstorm threatened from out at sea with its drum roll rumbling the sky, a bolt of lightning split the darkness, a thunderclap boomed and all the heavens opened up to join the scene. Then with a nod of the head, we were off and running to whatever fate might bring … sprinting like the devil to the jetty.

Unless you've ever been close enough to danger to have felt its hot foul breath scorch the hairs on the back of your neck, it is hard to imagine what can go through a man's mind when at any given moment fate might strike him down. But be that as it may, what happened next was not what we had planned, nor what we could have foreseen. Although my feet seemed to grow wings and carried me on with a swiftness I had not known that I had possessed, it soon became apparent that we would be requiring a lot more than speed to succeed, for a voice called *'halt'* then a musket fired, and Charlie was felled by a sentry's bullet while Tom Page made a dash for the trees.

Now the rest of us are here at the quarry a few miserable hours later, huddled up together 'neath an ancient eucalypt, trying in vain to shelter from the storm with each man clinging to his own dark thoughts, until all eyes turned in my direction when I opened up the bags. I found a piece of salted beef in one … five or six pounds at my reckoning. And an old iron kettle had come along for the ride, so I took off the lid and placed it out in the rain to catch what we could of some drinking water. We have some flour and what appears to have been a block of oatmeal biscuit, but it has been turned into sop by the unforgiving elements. When I opened up the second sack I found some more biscuit; a quantity of bread and a good deal of flour, but the whole damn lot has been spoiled like the first. So that is the full extent of what we now possess ... barely enough food to last three or four days; a kettle; a musket; a small amount of ammunition and a tinderbox to help us light a fire.

It's just those few items and not a damn thing more, except for what we are wearing on our backs. I lean back against a tree to try and gather my thoughts, and though I do not at this moment speak of how things look, I am burdened by the notion of what a sad and sorry foursome we must seem, all soaked as we are to the skin. And as I sit here feeling like a half-drowned rat, the saying: *'out of the frying pan and into the fire,'* drags its dark and gloomy countenance to my door. With my thoughts all scattered like leaves before the wind, there is no denying that the facts are as plain as can be ... a third of our men are gone, half of our food is spoiled, the weather gods are plotting against us and I doubt we'll be sleeping on a night like this.

It is now long past midnight at my estimation, and no more than a handful of words have passed between us, while the mood is dark and gloomy as a blind man's cell. We *had* planned to put as many miles as possible between the guards and ourselves, but in weather as foul as this, we have no choice but to stay where we are until the first light of dawn comes to show us the way.

Sodden to the skin and chilled to the bone, I try to reflect upon happier times and home. *Home* ... I manage to smile to myself at what thoughts the word conveys, but I will talk more of that when I feel up to the task.

I awoke from a fitful half-sleep to see that the storm had passed and my clothes were still clinging from the night's foul weather. Dawn was fast approaching and I was anxious to get underway. Though sore of head, stiff of limb and bone-weary beyond compare, I felt no need to dwell upon the night just passed so I wandered off to heed nature's call. On my return a short time later ... as if by dint of having read my thoughts, the others were up and showing eagerness to leave:

'We think we need to be on our way,' Bill was quick to suggest, before stressing the point: 'Our pursuers may well be close at hand,' and as we all seemed to be in agreement, I mentioned what was playing on my mind: 'I've been setting my head to some calculations,' as I picked up a stick and scratched the number 400 in the dirt at our feet. 'That is the number of nautical miles to Sydney town according to what mister Collins told me on the journey out, and a fit man can walk thirty or forty miles a day without even breaking into a sweat.'

Dan then piped up with some thoughts of his own: 'And if the task becomes a difficult one, twenty five miles a day is like a walk in the park.' While both George and Bill gave a nod of assent, I went on with making my point: 'If we were to take an average day's travel,' as I drew the number 30 in the dirt: 'Fourteen days ... or three weeks at most should see us somewhere close to our destination.'

I looked into their faces again and another nod from Bill had him say: 'A fortnight or so sounds a likely target,' before going on to add: 'And once there, we can mingle with the local populace until we can pick up a passage for home.'

He reached for the kettle ... half full of water from the overnight rain, took a draft from the spout then offered it around: 'And what of the food?' asked George as he looked with disdain at the state of the supplies: 'The meat will only last three or four days at most. Perhaps even less in the heat of the sun.' I glanced over to where Dan's musket was standing up against a tree: 'If Dan can manage to shoot enough game to meet our needs, the task can be achieved as long as the powder and shot holds out.' Dan quickly chipped in with the reassurance we all needed to hear: 'You have my word that I will make it so.' The ideas were coming thick and fast and we all had thoughts aplenty: 'If them savages can live off what they kill by hunting with little more than a pointy stick, men such as we are certain to catch more than enough game for the table.' Bill nodded his head in agreement:

'And there must be all sorts of fruits and berries growing out there in nature's larder.' It seemed that things were looking up. Moreover, judging by my comrades' behaviour, they appeared to be looking to me for the leadership role. I got to my feet and reached for the bag of supplies, and after we had broken our fast and the first rays of morning heralded their warning to get underway, I glanced down again at the numbers in the dirt: 'Sydney town is in the direction of the north east, of that much I am certain, for I had the opportunity of studying mister Collins' charts on the journey out while he was busy with other things.'

I pointed my finger towards the north east, then off to a hillock fading to grey far off in the hazy distance: 'If we aim today for yonder mountain and keep the bay to our left, by the close of day when we stop to eat, we should be able to sleep nice and easy when the sun goes down with a good day's travel behind us.

That was the way things stood, as sure as sure can be … we were off on our way to Lord-knows-where, with one thing we knew to be true: We were all free men again.[1]

---

[1] ***Footnote:***
Thomas Page *was captured by the guards the very next day, and while* **Charles Shore** *survived the musket wound, he was said to have drowned in 1815 when the schooner* ***'Geordy'*** *was lost at sea during a howling gale.*

CHAPTER 2

27ᵗʰ December, 1803

We were on our way to freedom, hugging the coastline, while the gentle terrain brought relief to our limbs and the warmth of the sun was the wind 'neath our wings as its golden glow lit up the sky. Having travelled thus for some ten miles or so, we stopped for a rest at a timbered bluff in the lee of some higher ground. From this lofty vantage point, we were able to look back on some twenty miles of coastline, espying in the distance our old ship *Calcutta* laying at anchor at Sullivan Bay. Looking no bigger than a child's toy, it was the ship we could see and not a thing more - not a boat, not a flag nor a sign of a redcoat anywhere to be seen:

'We seem to have outwitted them,' George was quick to boast as he passed us the kettle after taking a draft.

'Perhaps so,' said I: 'But I will rest a lot easier when I know that to be true.' We sat in the shade of a mighty gum tree while I shared out a portion of beef to all. And as I paused to reflect upon the morning thus far… the land had been flat and the going easy, but from the look of the terrain that lay ahead, there were hills up ahead of a much higher degree. If it had been left to me and to no one else, I would have been happy for some peace and quiet, but silence had never been a part of Dan's outgoing nature, and he got to his feet after having eaten his allocation: 'What say you all to me firing the musket?'

Firing it at *what?*' George asked. Dan pointed to a piece of dung lying on the ground: 'A creature of the wild has been here I would hazard to say. And not long ago by my estimate,' as he picked it up and studied it closely: 'See how fresh it is.'

George gave it little more than a cursory glance: 'A kangaroo I warrant,' … spoken like an expert on the subject which we knew he was not:

'Bloody hard to catch though. I only ever saw *one* brought back from a hunt during all our weeks at the settlement,' as he turned his attention from Dan to me: 'What say *you* to him firing the musket William?' I picked up the gun … closing one eye as I drew a bead along the barrel: 'As the weapon is untried, we will have to test its accuracy sooner or later.' Dan nodded his head in agreement:

'Yes, that is true. Suppose we were to come under attack from a party of savages? Not being aware of the weapon's peculiarities could very well cost us our lives.'

And to give further weight to the point he was making: 'And you never know …

I might get lucky and bring down a beast for our meat supply.' For some unknown reason, George felt the decision should be left to *me*: 'I think *you* should be the one to decide William.' This seemed as a good time as any to clear the air on the leadership point: 'Decisions that affect the four of us should not be made by one man alone,' while Bill was quick to agree: 'My thoughts in a nutshell. Any decisions should be *group* decisions,' as he glanced from Dan to the musket:

'I agree that we will need to test the gun, but rather than waste powder and shot on target practice, why not hold off until such time as we *do* happen across a creature of the forest?' adding as he glanced about for a place to relieve himself: 'And if we do not find game by day's end, perhaps we can *then* talk of target practice.' That seemed a perfect way to settle the issue, and I smiled to myself at his common-sense approach. I had liked Bill's style back in England and I liked it still. At the ripe old age of six and twenty ... not only does he happen to be three years my senior but he is a damn sight wiser, with a way of presenting an argument plain and simple that usually wins the day. However, it was then that I recalled how he'd conducted our own defence at the trial back home, and how we'd both been sent down with a guilty verdict, but I had long since forgiven that lapse of form with a saying I knew to be tried and true ... *'you cannot win them all.'*

The sun had long passed its zenith when I thought of Dan's words from when we'd first started out: *'twenty five miles a day is easy walking,'* for the terrain was now thick with ancient trees, and the climb that went with it was both long and exhausting in every degree.

The heat grew more intense as the day wore on ... shimmering bright like a spectre of light off through the summery haze. And when we arrived at a place where rocky crags and fern gullies green held an abundance of water from the last night's rain, we paused to rest once again. From the angle of the sun fading westward in the sky, we estimated our day's travel at some twenty or so miles as we sat on the trunk of a fallen tree while Dan had wandered off alone.

Ten minutes or so later, he rushed back in a flutter: 'I just saw a party of blacks.'

'Where?' asked I.

'Just over the ridge,' as he hastily pointed back in the direction of where he'd just come: 'Five or six of them there were, with their naked bodies all painted up like they were about to go to war with the devil himself,' said while puffing and panting as we sprang to our feet to follow: 'They were milling around, all armed to the teeth with shields and spears,' as he led the way onward with us at his heels. We came to a halt at the crest of the ridge, and saw not a thing but miles and miles of countryside punctuated by a meandering river at the bottom of the hill. George looked all about before turning to say so: 'I see no blacks.'

'But they were there as I described,' gasped Dan in disbelief: 'Just as plain as the nose on my face.'

'Did they see *you?*' asked I.

'No. I don't think so. I concealed myself behind a tree.'

The scene appeared tranquil in every way, until Bill spoilt the moment with a worrying thought: 'They could be watching us at this very moment. I have heard it said that they can appear and disappear right before your eyes.'

'I have heard that as well,' said I.

'So what do we do?' asked George, as he nervously looked about.

'We cannot stay up here,' said I, as I tried to gather my scattered thoughts while looking back in the direction from where we'd just come: 'This hill looks like the one we were aiming for when we started out this morning. So we are right on track for our first day's goal.' I looked to the river: 'and if we are going to get to Sydney town, we cannot allow ourselves to be put off at the first sign of danger.

'I agree,' said Bill: 'Unless we are of a mind to turn back now, we will have to cross that river before the sun goes down.'

'And what of the blacks?' George asked. Bill's reply was as sensible as ever:

'We knew from the outset that our venture was fraught with danger,' as he turned to look the rest of us fair and square in the eye: 'So I suggest we cross the river right here and now,' and after George and I nodded our heads in agreement, Bill turned to Dan with some sage advice: 'This could be as good a time as any to keep the musket primed and ready to fire.' It appeared we were all of the same mind once again, and as we moved off down the hill in single-file, we saw them appear from behind a clump of trees - six black males bearing spears and shields, painted for battle as Dan had described, and each one as naked as the day they were born. I had heard it said that the blacks could throw a spear through the eye of a needle, so I breathed a sigh of relief when Dan took aim and fired a round off over their heads. That was the situation in its entirety ... all over and done in a musket's flash, for they had up and disappeared in the blink of an eye.

'They are as slippery as ghosts,' George was quick to observe as we readied ourselves to cross over the river. I was occupied with taking off my boots, when Dan reached out and grabbed hold of my arm: 'William, I cannot do it.'

'You cannot do what?' asked I.

'I cannot cross. For I cannot swim.'

'Not at **all**?' asked Bill, as he strained at the task of removing his breeches.

'Not a stroke,' said Dan: 'Not even if my life depended upon it.'

George was a whole lot less than subtle as he hopped on one leg while pulling off a boot: 'Perhaps your life **does** depend upon it lad.'

Bill was trying his best to urge Dan on while keeping an eye on the trees:

'It's not be much more than thirty yards from bank to bank Dan. I feel *sure* that you can do it.' By then I had divested myself of everything except what God had given me, before wading on in to the middle of the stream: 'This is the deepest point Dan,' as I raised my arms up over my head: 'It only comes up to my chest. Just wade out to me and I will help you to cross to the other side.'

'But I fear I cannot do it,' he called in vain.

I watched Bill urging him on, while George aimed the gun in the direction of the trees: 'Come on lad. Let us get these clothes off, then we can all cross over together,' as he helped him to take off his boots.

Now three lily-white men ... each one as naked as new-born babes started wading on into the shallows: 'Leave the clothes there on the bank,' I called out to the others: 'and I will go back and get them when Dan has crossed over.'

'That's it lad,' I heard Bill say: 'We will see you're safe and sound,' and with the waters now lapping at the top of their shoulders, we met in the middle of the murky stream: 'Put your arms around my neck Dan,' and I carried him across to the other side.

Now as the remnants of daylight gave way to the night, we sat around the fire with bellies full but provisions low, discussing the wisdom of camping so near until Bill made the comment: 'This is their back yard, so it matters not whether we camped here or ten miles away. They would soon find us if they were of a mind to attack.' George had already formed *his* opinion as he nervously looked about: 'We will be a whole lot safer here by the fire than out there at night in the wilds of the bush.' So with the now-familiar smell of eucalyptus smoke drifting off into the looming night, Bill turned to Dan with more words of advice: 'Be sure to keep the musket at hand lad. We do not want any surprises creeping up out of the dark.'

I then turned to the others with a suggestion of my own: 'I move that we all take turns at keeping watch,' before I went on to ask: 'What say you all to a two hour watch per man?' And we all agreed on the following plan … one to keep watch while the other three slept, with the sentry to maintain the fire.

Dan had volunteered to take the first watch, and as the other two talked quietly amongst themselves, I lay back gazing into the patchwork of diamonds adorning the vault of the sky. I found it a strange and a wondrous sky… not at all like the constellations that my grandfather had pointed out to me in my formative years. I had been dwelling on thoughts of he and of home, when Dan came to my attention and I turned to him and asked: 'I have never known you to be so quiet Dan. Is everything alright?' His gaze had been locked upon the dancing flames:

'I was just thinking of when I was a boy back home.'

'What part of Ireland are you from Dan?' He took a moment before giving his reply: 'Ballimoney. It's up in the north country,' as his gaze turned back to the flickering fire. 'Do you miss it?' I asked.

'Yes. I miss it so bad that it breaks my heart.

All fell quiet again until he turned to me and said: 'William?'

'Yes, Dan.'

'I have been thinking.'

'Thinking about what?' He paused for a moment while gathering his thoughts:

'I have been thinking about all of them miles between us and Sydney town.'
'What about them miles Dan?' He stared back into the dancing flames:

'There must be a whole lot of rivers between here and there.'

I started to catch onto the gist of his thinking: 'I imagine there *are* Dan.'

He went awfully quiet before turning to face me once again: 'William, I want to tell you something,' as he paused while he sought the appropriate words: 'When I was a lad. I was five I think. And my little brother Sean a mere eighteen months.' I watched him wipe away a tear: 'He was just at the stage of starting to walk,' as sadness came to settle and he sighed once more: 'He had a habit of finding his way into every nook and cranny.' Long used to Dan's light-hearted ways, this was a side to him I had not seen before, and he stared off into the night with tears in his eyes: 'I was supposed to watch out for him whenever mother was busy with her chores.' I watched him struggling to get the words out, so I held my tongue and waited: 'I only went out to check on the pups. It was not my intention to leave him alone.' I began to feel the gravity of where this was leading, as his eyes welled up with a million tears: 'They found him floating face-down in the pond.'

The only words I could manage were: '*Sorry Dan,*' but he was caught up in his grief and he heard me not: 'He must have lifted the latch after seeing me go.'

Once again I tried my best: 'I am very sorry Dan,' while his emotions overflowed and the tears ran down his cheeks: 'I was not gone more than a few minutes ... just a few lousy minutes was all it took.' He eyes locked onto the blazing coals:

'I have never been able to forgive myself William.'

All I could do was sit there in silence.

'I could never go near that pond again William.'

'Is that why you were so scared of crossing the creek Dan?'

'Yes.'

As a dark shroud of melancholy draped its gloomy cloak over this sad southern night, I returned to the place of my *own* secret thoughts, and neither he nor I said another thing more.

I awoke to the sound of the first birds' call, with the early dawn trying its level best to chase away the sadness from the night before. Embers were fading and turning to ash, as George threw a log on to give it a lift. 'Good morning,' said I, and he returned my greeting as I got to my feet.

'Anything to speak of from last night's watch?'

'Not a thing,' said he: 'All was quiet I am glad to report.'

Upon hearing that, I had wandered off alone to heed nature's call, and it was there by the shore that I saw what I saw … several bare footprints imprinted in the sand, no doubt left since the last high tide, so I rushed back to camp just as fast as I could go: 'Made within the hour I would estimate.'

Bill sprang to his feet: 'I think it prudent to leave at once and not waste precious minutes on breaking our fast.'

'Dan, is the musket primed?' I asked, as we readied ourselves for travel.

'All primed and ready to fire,' came his response.

So we set off as one to follow the shore with the sun rising off to our right … travelling mile after mile through low-lying marsh, till hunger and thirst got the better of fear, and an exhausted Dan finally stopped to ask: 'What say you all to our resting a while? I fear I am ready to drop.'

While the others sat on a fallen tree, I opened up the bag for all to see: 'This meal and perhaps one more,' said I. Not much more could be said on the subject … a mere morsel now and another one at sundown would see out the last of our food supply. And as I passed around a piece for each, Bill pointed to some water birds swimming on a pond: 'Do you suppose you could hit one of *those* Dan?'

'I could certainly give it a try,' he replied.

After easing the gun into the crook of his shoulder and taking aim along the barrel … the blast that followed sent every water bird that could lay claim to the name soaring on high to the heavens. And as the sky settled back to the way it had been, George reached for the gun and looked it over: 'Where did you get it?'

'It was Fosbrook's,' Dan replied, as he puffed out his chest and added as he did so: 'I relieved him of it when his back was turned.' George chuckled in amusement as he handed it back: 'I'm surprised it didn't blow up in your face,' then he chuckled again: 'That explains why there was no report of a stolen gun.'

'What do you mean?' Dan meekly asked.

George had a smug grin from ear to ear: 'Everyone at Sullivan Bay knew that Fosbrook's old weapon couldn't hit the side of a barn.'

Dan's pride was deflated in one fell swoop, so I thought it best to go to his aid: 'Never mind Dan. If it shoots it can kill. That's all we need to worry about.'

After we'd made short work of the dwindling rations and George had swatted his third mosquito in as many minutes, he hauled himself to his blistered feet:

'If we stay here much longer we will be eaten alive by these damned insects,'as he picked up the kettle to take out his frustration on the first thing he saw:

'I'm sick and tired of lugging this thing around. I see no point when we have no tea for the pot,' and he tossed it away just as far as he could.

Needless to say, things at this point were far from harmonious as we moved on listless and low. It was near mid-morning when we came to a gully just as a flock of white parrots took off from the trees … their yellow crowns catching the sun.

And as we paused for a moment at the edge of that gorge, we noticed four black females poking about by a meandering creek, and each one was as naked as a new born babe. Chattering away in their own queer tongue, they were up to their knees in amongst the reeds, while three little children were frolicking about in innocent glee. It was a heart-warming scene I have to confess, but when one of them pointed in our direction, they dashed out of sight in the blink of an eye.

We hastened down the embankment to the water's edge, where an old fallen tree trunk lay straddling the creek, seemingly placed there to make crossing the stream a simple affair.

'What do you think they were doing?' George asked, with a smirk on his face at what he'd just witnessed. 'They looked like they were fossicking about for something in the mud,' came Bill's reply.

'And they might be alerting their menfolk to our presence at this very moment,' said I, as we came to our senses and hurried on over the log.

With another hour's travel under our belts, and the coastal fringe having given way to a mighty forest of ancient trees, I was looking up into one of those giants … all wrapped up in thoughts of my own, when a musket blast shattered the air. 'For Christ's sake,' George yelled: 'Give us some warning before you fire that thing.' Dan pointed off through the trees as the smoke from the gunpowder started to clear: 'There was a big grey kangaroo watching us, bold as brass the bloody thing was,' as he hurried off to investigate. We looked at each other and were just about to follow when he turned back all sad and forlorn. 'Did you hit it?' we asked as one. 'No,' he meekly replied: 'I seem to have missed him by a whisker.'

No longer in the mood for playful banter, George made advances in Dan's direction: 'You'd be better off using the bloody thing as a club next time,' and he tried to snatch it away: 'Give it to me, it's about as useful as the bloody kettle was.' Dan was stubborn and kept his resolve, but George was just as determined to get his way: 'I said give it to me,' as he tried to wrest it out of

Dan's firm grip. George was showing a side to his nature that I had not seen before, and with Dan seemingly just as prepared to hold his ground, I thought it best if I intervene:

'Leave it be George,' but he seemed determined to win the day:

'I'm going to smash that useless excuse for a firearm into a million pieces,' as his lip curled into a horrible sneer.

I had never gone looking for trouble in all my years, but I had never shirked an issue and was not about to start at *this* stage of life: 'I said leave it be George.' And as an awkward pause froze the moment in time, George finally saw the sense in backing down, and he released his grip then walked away.

Things had settled down for the moment, but they were far less happy than those first few days, and a darn sight worse was about to follow.

The sun was receding below the tree line when we came face to face with what Dan had been dreading, for a vast river mouth lay directly in our path... meandering down to the endless sea. Not a word had been uttered since the musket incident, but Bill changed all that when he stated the obvious:

'That will take a power of effort to get across.'

I took a look up at the gloomy sky: 'It will be dark soon. Perhaps we should make camp here and look for a way to cross the river tomorrow.'

Bill had lit the fire after we had all done our bit for the wood supply, and with the night creeping in and spreading its cloak in ever-lengthening shadows, the mood was as low as a lizard's belly, for the food was nearly gone and our plans seemed as stable as shifting sands.

I lay that night with my own dark thoughts, till I was awoken at dawn by a shake of the arm: 'What is it Dan?'

'William, I cannot go on.'

'What do you mean, you cannot go on?'

'I have made up my mind to go back.'

'Back where? asked I.

'Back to the settlement,' came his reply.

I glanced at the other two asleep by the fire: 'Have you told them yet?'

'No, not yet. I wanted to tell you first.'

I looked him fair and square in the eye: 'Are you sure Dan?'

'Yes. Just as sure as I will ever be.'

Toward the middle of that overcast morning ... a mile or two further upstream, three sodden figures trudged out of the river, before continuing on their way.[2]

---

[2] ***Footnote.***
Dan had been gone for over a week when he staggered back into the settlement ... footsore and leg-weary and as grubby as a chimney-sweep, and the musket was returned to its rightful owner.

CHAPTER 3

30ᵀᴴ DECEMBER, 1803

I was beginning to wonder just how many rivers we would have to contend with, for it was barely an hour since we'd forded the last, and we were once again faced with crossing another. But we managed the undertaking and were sitting there drying our clothes by the fire, talking over how things stood: 'You cannot help but see the funny side of all these rivers,' said Bill as he smiled with a touch of irony. 'What do you mean?' asked George as he tossed another stick onto the fire: 'What were our jailers thinking of, deciding to settle at Sullivan Bay when there is hardly any water and not enough soil to even grow a split pea?'

He gazed about at the surrounding terrain: 'Yet up here... little more than two day's march away, there are rivers to spare and good soil aplenty.' He scooped up a handful of rich brown earth and watched it run through his weather-beaten fingers: 'Take a look at this soil. You could poke a stick into the ground anywhere around here and it would grow into a tree before the sun went down.'

He then glanced up into the overcast sky: 'Speaking of the sun William … I tried to get a bead on where it rose this morning to help us to gauge our direction.'

'I know. I tried the same thing,' I replied: 'But it was too hard to tell through the thick haze and the cloud cover.'

The land was flat for as far as the eye could see, with the terrain to our right leading to three prominent mountains standing blue and tall off in the hazy distance: 'I think we should stick to our original plan and aim for the hills while keeping the bay to our left,' as I looked to the others for confirmation:

'What are your thoughts on the matter?'

George was the first one to give a reply:

'I'm starting to think we are *already* lost. Those hills are not the ones that we were aiming for when we first started out.' Bill was quick though to take my side:

'Well do you have a better idea?' George merely gave a shrug of the shoulders:

'I don't give a damn which way we go, just as long as there's food to be had.' Right on cue at the mention of food, a herd of kangaroo appeared on the scene as they paused at our flank to graze. 'Bastards,' cursed George: 'It's as if they have come here to tease us,' as a big old red … six feet tall if an inch started chewing on the grass without a care in the world: 'It's as if he can tell how hungry we are and is thumbing his nose at our predicament.' George picked up a stick and feigned to throw it in their direction and they casually hopped away. Bill gave a sigh as he reached for his clothes: 'There's no denying it,' as he got to his feet and put on his trousers: 'We *do* need to think about the food situation.'

'There must be *something* we can eat around here,' George muttered as he pulled on his boots: 'How do the blacks manage?' As usual, Bill had a theory that was brimful of wisdom: 'They've learned by trial and error over thousands of years as to what can be eaten and what cannot.' That's when I followed up with a thought of my own: 'Perhaps we should all spread out and look around, then we can meet back here to share out what we've found.' George was becoming more and more contrary by the minute: 'And just what is it you expect us to find?'

'Anything that might be edible,' I replied.

'And if it turns out that it *cannot* be eaten?' he asked with a large dose of sarcasm. 'Then we can worry about that when the time comes.'

We each headed off in different directions while staying within sight of the campfire smoke, and I was poking about near the trunk of a tree when a small brown snake slithered past my boot before disappearing under a sheet of bark.

I hasten to mention my dislike of snakes, but I did my bit for the food situation and dispatched the reptile to kingdom-come. And when I carried its limp body back to the camp, George was there watching as I dropped it by the fire.

'Is it a lizard?' he asked.

'A snake,' I replied. He sneered as he came over for a closer look:

'Seems a shame to have taken it away from its mother.'

'All the more for Bill and I if that is how you feel.' Just as I had uttered the words, Bill reappeared from out of the scrub: 'How did you fare?' I enquired.

He held out some mushrooms he'd happened across: 'I am not sure whether they are toadstools or not, but I decided to pick them nonetheless. What of you two?'

George gave a shrug of the shoulders: 'All I could find was a dead opossum.'

'And where is it?'

'It was crawling with maggots so I left it there.'

I drew Bill's attention to the snake at my feet. 'Is it a lizard?' he asked.

'A snake,' I replied.

'And what of the poison?' asked a dubious George. I took a wild guess ... hoping to God what I was about to say would turn out to be true: 'I think it will be safe enough to eat if the head is first removed.' And with the embers now giving off a golden glow, I placed it the dead reptile on top of the coals. Being in one of his reflective moods as we waited for the snake to cook, Bill leant back against the trunk of a tree and casually made the comment: 'It's a queer place this land they brought us to,' as he pointed to the strips of bark hanging off the trunk:

'So strange how the trees here keep their *leaves* while shedding their bark the way they do.' He then gazed off into the virgin bush: 'And so weird how the creatures of the wild carry their young about in a pouch the way that they do.' George had his mind on *other* things though, and he dragged the snake from the coals: 'I would say that it's as ready as it's ever going to be.'

After breaking the shrunken creature into three equal portions, I handed a piece to each. It was a tasty treat I have to admit, like something akin to chicken, but it had barely touched the sides when George glanced went over and looked at the mushrooms: 'What do you propose we do with these?'

It seemed like Bill was about to try for himself, when he picked one up for closer inspection: 'They look a little doubtful, but you never can tell ... they might just happen to be tasty and full of nutrition,' before screwing up his nose and adding the point: 'But then again they might be poisonous,' and he put it back down with the others. Nothing more was said on the subject for a minute or so, until Bill appeared to have made up his mind that it was now or never:

'They were growing in abundance so if they *can* be eaten, it would be helpful to our cause to know one way or the other,' as he picked up a twig and looked both George and I fair and square in the eye: 'Why not draw straws to see which one of us gets to try one?' then he turned his back and snapped the twig in three different-sized pieces. I nervously watched him hold out his hand, with three ominous sticks protruding from the side of his fist: 'Who would like to go first?'

After George stepped forward and took a piece, that left me to have to sadly do the same. Unfortunately for me, when I looked at *mine* then at the other two pieces, there was no denying the outcome: 'I never *did* like mushrooms,' said I, as I picked one up and looked it over. It *appeared* to be a mushroom, although it was yellowy brown and ugly to boot. I gave it a sniff to see how it smelt, but that gave no indication to help me decide. It felt soft to the touch ... a little clammy perhaps, like the frogs I had caught in the pond as a boy. There was only one way to find out, so boots and all ... I swallowed it down, barely pausing to chew.

All seemed fine for a minute or two until my head started spinning and I dropped to my knees. And as an almighty cramp tied my stomach in knots, multi-coloured lights flashed bright before my eyes. They later described how I'd frothed at the mouth - how I'd started trembling all over and collapsed in a heap, and how they'd covered me over and kept me warm, hoping for the worst to pass. I recall very little of what took place, save for heaving and retching till I thought I would die. But an hour or so later I was back among the living – feeling worse for wear but a great deal wiser. We were back under way when I could manage to walk, though I was dragging my feet with an aching head and I was so damn hungry I could have eaten my boot, if only I had one to spare. And while the sun kept up its solitary path ... making slow pace as always towards the horizon, we happened upon a rippling stream where we finally elected to camp for the night.

Though we'd gathered wood aplenty and lit up a fire, there were no hearty discussions to lighten the moment, just three empty stomachs, a heap of dark thoughts and a power of misery for each man to endure. Not even when night finally fell, bringing along with it a whole sky full of stars ... not that nor the hearty glow of the fire could stave off the gloom.

George had slunk off on his own to keep his own counsel, and as I lay back gazing at that sky full of diamonds, Bill turned to me and posed the question:

'Do you think we are still on course for Sydney town?' He seemed to have been reading my very own thoughts: 'I am inclined to admit I am having doubts.'

And as the crickets joined in with the sounds of the bush, Bill let out the saddest of sighs: 'I am beginning to think I will never see England again,' before pausing for a moment then choosing to add: 'I had a dream last night William.'

'What was it about?' asked I.

'About England and home,' as his eyes grew misty while he gazed into the flames:

'I was on board a ship bound for England and had just finished packing up my trunk as we got closer to the shore.' I lay there trying to visualize the scene … wondering how it would feel to be on *my* way home, then hearing his voice again brought me back to the moment: 'We were ever so near to the cliffs of Dover that I could almost touch their chalky whiteness.' He took his time before adding:

'But the cursed wind kept blowing us further and further away from the land.'

He went quiet again, locked up in the prison of his own sad thoughts:

'Then when the sun finally came up and they dropped the anchor, I looked out through the porthole and found to my dismay that we were back at Sullivan Bay.' Though heavy of heart with my *own* set of doubts, I did what I could to try and cheer him up: 'We will get to see England again, I feel sure of it.' He turned to me with a most melancholy smile: 'Thanks William,' as he rolled onto his side to face the fire. There are many strange mysteries to this ancient southern land … things that make words seem small and a man even smaller, and neither he nor I said another thing more.

When the sun began to rise upon our fourth day of freedom, I awoke to the chill of a burnt out fire, before I headed off to heed nature's call. And as I squatted on my haunches by a giant of a tree - trying to give all my attention to the job at hand, a bird started pecking at its gnarly old trunk, and I was soon rushing back to relay what I'd seen: 'If a bird can eat tree sap, perhaps *we* can too.' Bill was quick to join me in my moment of glee: 'Yes. I heard it said at Sullivan Bay that the natives eat it mixed with water,' while George expressed his usual contrary view:

'I'd rather take my chances with the mushrooms.' Just as he'd spoken, the first golden rays of sunlight appeared over the horizon and it was then that we made an alarming discovery: 'Look at where the sun is rising. It seems that the grey skies of yesterday had us mistakenly heading in the wrong direction.'

As the others saw *too* the mistake we had made, I scratched my whiskered chin with a world-weary sigh: 'Me thinks we will be needing to revise our travel plans.' Bill looked back in the direction from which we had come, in an effort to sum up the situation: 'If we were to go back to our original course, all we would be doing was covering the same ground as yesterday.' For once George chose to agree: 'And we *know* there's no food to be had if we make that choice.'

Bill turned around to ask *my* opinion: 'What do you think we should do?'

I thought for a moment, then pointed to where the distant bay lay glistening bright like a mirror of light far off through the haze of the morning:

'I think our best chance of finding food is to head back toward the sea.'

Even George nodded his head in agreement: 'It appears to be our only chance. What is the good of aiming for Sydney town if we starve to death along the way?'

'Then we are all in agreement,' Bill declared: 'We head south to the bay and then follow the shore till there is food to be had.' So the decision was made and we changed our course, still hungry and far from home.

The hours dragged on through another long day, and though all of our thoughts may have been as one, George was the one who chose to complain: 'My stomach feels like my throat has been cut. Surely there is *something* to eat around here.'

We were knee-deep in marshes just a mile from the bay, where an abundance of sea birds made the skies their own, with their raucous cries filling the air:

'I wonder where they nest,' Bill paused to muse as we watched them riding the off-shore breeze. 'What does it matter *where* they nest?' George snapped... still looking for an excuse to grumble and moan. 'It matters because they are birds,' Bill was quick to reply: 'And where you find birds you will usually find nests. So it stands to reason that if you locate their nests, you have every chance of finding their eggs.' Bill had a point there I was inclined to agree, but once again George chose a negative view:

'How can there be nests when there is not a tree to be seen for miles?'

'Perhaps they nest among the reeds,' said I. So with our boots squelching mud every step that we took, we searched the reeds for an hour or more until weary and footsore once again, we abandoned the marshes where they met up with the sea. And there on the shore of and endless bay … still hot and bothered with nothing to show, we paused for a rest without saying a word and sat 'neath the shade of a tree. I had been sitting there gazing out to sea, all tied up in my own solitary thoughts, when George chose the moment to pipe up again:

'We cannot just sit here doing nothing. If I don't get a drink soon I am sure I will perish. There must be fresh water around here *somewhere*.' Bill had been setting his mind toward the distant coastline and pointed in the direction of where he was looking: 'See that rocky headland off in the distance. See where it meets the ocean? I doubt that it is much more than ten miles at best,' as he sought our response while making his point: 'If we were to make for there before the sun goes down, we may well get lucky and find a stream along the way. And who knows? - we might even find some shellfish while we follow the shore.'

With no better idea of my own to offer, Bill had *my* vote: 'Yes, why not? They say that fortune favours the brave.' So we hugged the shore on a receding tide, sweltering through the heat of the long afternoon, until weak and weary and on the verge of exhaustion, we were blessed once again by a life-giving stream flowing miraculously there before us.

Another river crossed when we had slaked our thirst, and we came out of the water on the opposite bank to be confronted there and then by an alien vision.

'What are they?' George asked, as we stood dripping water from head to toe. 'They appear to be Aboriginal huts,' I replied: 'And long-since abandoned by the look of them.' There were five in total - all resembling the other made from bark and reeds, and each large enough to sleep a party of four. They'd been erected around the perimeter of a central fireplace, encircled by rocks for a hearth.

'It's been quite some time since *this* felt the warmth of a flame,' said I as I bent down and touched the ash: 'Weeks or even months if I were to hazard a guess.'

George had just noticed something else, and brought our attention to a mound of shells: 'Look yonder,' said he: 'It appears to be one of those middens like the ones they discovered at Sullivan Bay.'

'And a big one at that,' added Bill, as the three of us approached for a closer look. I picked up a mussel shell - long since faded to a ghostly-white by the unforgiving rays of the summer sun: 'It must have taken generations to amass so many.'

The site we had stumbled upon was on a level piece of ground perched well above the high-water mark, flanked on one side by the river, and on the other … by the headland Bill had pointed out in the distance earlier that morning.

'They seem to have chosen an ideal location,' said I: 'Not only does it offer an abundance of fresh water, but judging by the size of this midden, whoever was living here had a regular source of shellfish as well.' George however was his doubting self: 'If it's such an ideal place, why would they leave?'

'Because like everything else in nature,' came Bill's response: 'shellfish are seasonal,' adding as he glanced about at the surrounding terrain: 'I don't know about *these* natives, but from what has been discovered about other indigenous tribes from around the world, they always leave enough of a sustainable food source to maintain the survival of the species long after they've gone.' He stared up to the top of the mound… piled head and shoulders above the height of a man: 'and judging by the size of *this* one, they've been coming here for many a year.' As he gazed up at the pile he added the thought: 'They are sure to return when the time is right.' Still dripping water from head to toe, I chose the moment to make a suggestion: 'I feel it would serve us well to spend the night here.'

'I agree,' Bill replied: 'For if the natives *were* still in the vicinity, they would not have abandoned the site so readily.' George's mind was on his stomach again:

'Then let's search the shallows while the tide is low and see for ourselves if there is food to be had.'

We were knee deep in water once again, searching the rocks pools with nothing to show, except for hundreds upon hundreds of black mussel shells just starting to grow as they clung for dear life onto the tidal rocks. Noticing how tiny they were, Bill made the comment: 'These are even too small for a starving man.'

'No bigger than my thumbnail,' came my response. But George cared not a lick that they were lacking in size and was busily chipping off all he could manage: 'Better small than none at all,' said he, as he carried an armful back to shore to smash them open with a stone. 'Come on,' he called from the beach: 'Try some for yourselves,' and as he sat there on the sand feeding his face, we reluctantly joined in the farce. Although now well on its way toward the western horizon, the sun was growing more oppressive with each passing hour, and while we sat in the shade of a big old tree, the air rang loud with every screeching insect God had ever created … all having come together to take part in the cacophony of sound. Having grown tired of just sitting around, George got to his feet once again: 'Damned shellfish have made me thirsty. All that effort and there was barely enough in them to keep a flea alive,' as he headed off down to the river.

When the sun had disappeared and darkness had fallen, and all the heavens started showing off their wonderland of stars, not one of us showed an interest in the beautiful display, for there were more pressing things playing on our minds. George had settled down into one of the huts as the sound of the crickets took over the night, and as I sat by the fire thinking of home, Bill was there beside me staring into the flames: 'I wonder what tomorrow will bring,' he said as he threw another branch onto the fire. And as I watched the sparks climb out of sight into the gathering night, Bill revealed what was playing on his mind: 'I have to admit that I would welcome the guards with open arms if they were to appear at this moment from out of the bush.' When I offered no comment to support his view, he returned to his solitary thoughts, and as I looked up to watch a shooting star blazing a trail across the heavens, Bill attempted to engage me again: 'William?'

'Yes Bill.' He turned his eyes back to the glow of the fire:

'My mind is leaning toward thoughts of turning back.'

'Turning back to what?' He continued to stare into the flames:

'I feel if we were to make it back to Sullivan Bay and hand ourselves in, we could eventually earn the right to become free settlers.'

'And what of the lash?' asked I. He turned to look into my doubting eyes:

'If the price of freedom is a flogging, it is a price I would pay every day of the week.' He then retreated into silence when I gave my reply:

'I am sorry Bill but I will not turn back.'

When the sun broke through upon our sixth day of freedom, I opened my eyes to see Bill gazing up into the foliage of a tree and he noticed me stir as I got to my feet: 'Morning,' said he. As I returned his greeting, he pointed to a bird sitting high up in a branch: 'Would you say that is a magpie William?' Having just awoken from a fitful sleep I thought the question strange, but replied in the affirmative: 'Yes. I believe it is.' He smiled the smile of an innocent child as he continued to gaze up into the tree: 'There was one just like it back home when I was a boy.

It used to fly into our yard and land on the fence almost every afternoon.'

The bird started warbling a beautiful tune ... bringing a touch of joy to the sounds of the bush: 'But our English magpies look somewhat different and they do not sing as sweetly as the ones that live here.' He then turned to me and asked: 'Have you noticed that?' When I once more said yes, Bill gazed in the bird's direction again: 'I will always have a special place in my heart for a magpie.' When George finally arose from a night spent indoors, with the three of us now all up and about, I thought it a good time right to confirm our plans, so I turned to the others and asked: 'Are we still in agreement about following the coast?'

George seemed more forlorn than his usual self: 'We don't seem to have a choice. But of one thing I am certain, if we don't eat soon it will make no difference *which* way we go.'

Back and travelling once again, we were making slow pace as we climbed the headland, trudging on weary and low. And with no conversation to help pass the time, we made our way on up the timbered bluff without a single word spoken between us. Then as we got to the top and espied the view, one could not help but marvel at the rugged shore of this ancient coast, stretching westward and beyond for as far as the eye could see: 'This land could be a paradise beyond compare,' mused a wistful Bill as the three of us took in the glorious scene.

But when he added the words: 'Were it not for the lack of food to sustain us,' we were once more reminded of the task ahead, and of our perilous situation.

Having set off again while we followed the ridge, we trudged on wearily through the heat of the day, all mournfully silent as if the weight of the world were upon our shoulders, and when we got to the stage where we could barely take another step more, we stopped in the shade for a well-earned rest.

While I nodded off there at the base of a tree, Bill handed me a berry he'd just picked from a bush: 'Do you think this could be edible?' It was a light shade of purple - a little soft when I squeezed, and no bigger than the size of a child's fingernail: 'I have no idea,' came my response as I recalled the mushrooms from earlier days before quickly handing it back. George got to his feet and walked off in a huff, saying with a sneer as he did so: 'Why don't you try it and see?'

Bill had thrown the berry away, and while we sat there in silence at the base of the tree, we heard George call out from off through the trees: 'A ship, a ship, I've just seen a ship,' as he hurried back gasping for breath.

'Are you sure?' we asked as we sprang to our feet:

From Dreamtime to Armageddon

'Yes, I saw it with my very own eyes,' as he eagerly bid us to follow.

'Did you see a flag?' I asked as we hurried along beside him.

'No, it was too far away to tell. But I am almost certain it was British.'

When we got to the top of a treeless hill, we saw the vessel in question lying at anchor just across the channel from the very spot upon which we were standing, and as we shielded our eyes from the glare of the sun, the truth then revealed itself for all to see: 'Do you see what I see?' I asked the others in stunned disbelief as I checked my bearings then checked them again: 'Unless I'm imagining things, that yonder hill in the distance is Arthur's Seat.'

Bill quickly picked up the gist of what I was saying: 'My goodness. I think it is.'

'And the ship,' said I, 'I am almost certain it is one of the ships that carried us out here from England.'

It was indeed ... lying there at anchor some ten miles or so west of the Collins Bay Settlement, and a mere three or four miles across the bay from where the three escapees were now staring in amazement at what they were seeing.

The ship's crew were taking on a supply of sandstone, and would continue to do so for four more days, before taking their load back to Sullivan Bay.

Buckley shook his head in disbelief. It seemed they'd trekked six long days from sunrise till dusk, only to have travelled almost full-circle around the bay to end up a stones-throw away from the redcoats from whom they had made their escape. Be that as it may, George was so excited he could barely stand still: 'It's a miracle. I feel our rescue is at hand,' and for once Bill agreed with what he was saying:

'I feel you are right, and we have no time to lose. Don't forget that on the day we escaped, our captors were already in the process of preparing to pack up and move the settlement to Van Diemen's Land,' as he turned to George with fire of enthusiasm ablaze in his eyes: 'We need to gather as much wood as we can so we can light a beacon to get their attention.' In spite of how excited

George had become, he again let his negative side come to the fore: 'Look how far away they are though. How will we possibly get their attention? Even if we were to light the mother of all fires, I fear it is too far away for our smoke to be seen.'

'A few miles it may be,' said Bill with an idea starting to form: 'But it would be one less mile if we were to light up the beacon fire over there,' as he pointed to an island lying just off-shore: 'If we can wade over to there when the tide is low, it would bring us that much closer to the ship, and increase our chances of them seeing our smoke.' As the three of us headed off down to the shore, Bill had one more try at winning me over: 'I feel that our luck might have turned for the better William. Will you not change your mind now that the chance of our rescue may be close at hand?' A part of me wanted to do as he asked, but the rest of me chose to resist: 'I'm sorry Bill, but I will not wait around to greet them if they send a boat across.' While we'd been talking, George hurried off ahead to the water's edge … calling for the two of us to follow: 'Hurry up. The tide is going out. It appears to be shallow enough for us to wade across.'

We'd taken off our boots and rolled up our trousers, before wading out to the reeds that defended the island from the range of the tides. Then after squelching through mud and up onto the shore, we'd soon amassed a pile of driftwood atop a tall scrubby hill. Having completed the task as best we could, Bill's directed his attention back to the ship with a new sense of hope: 'We'll set it alight when the sun goes down.'

Bill lit up the fire at the first sign of darkness, and as we sat around watching the glow of the flames, a storm blew in from out at sea and thunder-claps threatened the sky: 'That will be the end of the fire if a storm hits,' and as we retreated to the shelter of a nearby tree when the rain started falling, Bill turned to us with a worried look: 'Something just occurred to me … even if they *do* see the glow of our fire, I fear they may think it is only the fire from a native camp.'

George was aghast at the thought: 'My God I had not thought of that. If they *do* think it is only a fire that the blacks have lit, they would no more send a boat than fly to the moon.' I have to admit that the same notion had occurred to *me* some minutes earlier, and I'd already thought of a solution:

'Why not attach your shirts to the top of a tree then? and when they see the smoke and aim their telescope for a closer look, there will be no doubt as to who we are when they see your convict shirts flapping in the breeze.' George was overjoyed at my suggestion:

'Of *course,*' he beamed with a burst of enthusiasm, and with pelting rain now hissing at the sputtering coals, he said one more thing before we all battened down for a stormy night: 'At the first sign of clear weather when the sun comes up, we should light another fire and hang up our shirts from the highest tree.' One more bolt of lightning brought another clap of thunder, and all the heavens opened up to douse the flames.

The early warmth of the rising sun was heralding the start of another new day as I dragged my weary bones from my sodden bed of leaves to face our seventh day of freedom. Bill had been up since before the dawn, and as George crawled out from under a bush, Bill drew our attention to the nearest tree: 'You've not wasted any time,' George beamed with a grin from ear to ear. Bill was all smiles as well: 'It should flap about when the wind picks up,' before he went on to add:

'And I have some *further* news to tell … I found a pond when I went for a pee.'

He pointed his finger off through the scrub: 'A mere hundred yards from here.

It tastes a little brackish but is drinkable nonetheless.'

Although the day started out full of hope and promise, as the morning dragged on and the shadows shortened, in spite of the fact that our fire had been shrouding the sky in a blanket of smoke, no response from the ship was forthcoming.

And as every waiting moment dragged wearily by, George's impatience finally got the better of him: 'What's the matter with them? Even a blind man could see our smoke,' as he got to his feet and stormed away. Now that the two of us were on our own, Bill turned his attention to me again: 'I feel certain they will send a boat to rescue us before the day is out.'

'You may be right,' I replied, though I sensed he had more to say on the subject.

'I feel sure if we were to give ourselves up there is every chance that they would show leniency toward us.'

'They might at that,' I replied as I readied myself for his next attempt.

'Will you not reconsider William?' I almost gave in and changed my mind as he looked at me with his pleading eyes, but as my customary dogged nature refused to budge, I once again reverted to my old stubborn ways: 'I'm sorry Bill. But I have made up my mind that I will not go back.' It seems that I was not the *only* one who knew how to be stubborn, for Bill dug his heels in harder than ever:

'Now that we have come to experience just how unforgiving this country can be, I feel sure that if you do not come back you will surely die of starvation or be speared by the blacks.' But my blind determination refused to be swayed: 'That is a chance I am prepared to take.' He seemed to be weighing up whether to try one more time, till he let out a sigh and reached for his boots: 'Well at least we agree on *one* thing ... if we don't eat soon we will *all* perish.'

Bill and I had gone off again in search of food, but the closest we got was when a pair of grey ducks appeared on the pond. To our dismay however - the nearer we got, the faster they swam and as we watched them take wing and fly away, we were once again left empty-handed with nothing to show.

We traipsed back to the fire still hungry and low: 'Any sign of activity from the ship?' Bill asked, as we saw George sitting there like a picture of misery.

'None at all,' he replied: 'And it is unlikely there *will* be any time soon, for the wind has got stronger and is dispersing the smoke.'

'Perhaps they are waiting for calmer conditions,' said I, and at the very same moment I had chosen to speak, George jumped to his feet like a jack-in-box: 'Look,' said he: 'Do my eyes deceive me or are they lowering a longboat?'

Bill had started running down to the water's edge to greet them, and as George began to follow hot on his heels, I thought of taking my leave for the cover of the trees, but as I turned for a moment to watch the boat pitching and tossing as it tried making its approach through ever-worsening seas, the crew turned the boat around then rowed back to the ship.

By the time the sun had set on that fateful day, a dark sense of foreboding had invaded our camp and it seemed determined to stay. Having become obsessed with maintaining the fire, George was piling on branches like a man possessed... getting well and truly under Bill's skin in the process: 'It's no use wasting our wood supply George. It's not the fire that's the problem, any fool could tell that they've already *seen* our smoke.'

'Then what *should* I do Bill?' as his eyes lit up like the fires of hell: 'You're the one with an answer for everything. Why don't *you* tell us why the boat turned back?'

Although the ship was still anchored there three days later … to my fellow escapees' dismay on our tenth day of freedom … right before our eyes while we watched in surprise, the crew raised the anchor and the ship sailed away.

I lay listening to the chorus of a million bullfrogs on that final night, until the following morning saw George preparing to leave: 'What are you doing?'

'Going back,' he replied without so much as a glance in my direction.

'Are you going to wait for Bill?'

'No. I've made up my mind to travel alone.'

Right at that moment, Bill appeared from out of the scrub and having heard the tail end of our conversation, he turned to George and asked: 'Are you leaving?' George merely nodded as he pulled on his boots.

'Do you not think that it would be wiser to go together?' It was plain to see however that George had made up his mind: 'We would be at each other's throats before the sun went down if we continue to travel together.' And after picking up a smouldering stick out of the fire, he uttered the last words I was to ever hear him say: 'Good luck to you both,' then he turned and walked away.

As the morning gave way to the afternoon, Bill was the next one preparing to leave: 'Have you thought about where you will go William?'

I looked back across the water to where we'd first laid eyes on the ship:

'I thought I'd continue to follow the coast westward,' before adding: 'I remember Mister Collins talking of how sealers often come to these shores in search of prey. Who knows? I might just happen upon one of their hunting parties and be rescued.'

He smiled a sad and a lonely smile: 'I hope so William, I really do.'

He turned his attention to the sun in the sky: 'There are still a few hours of daylight left,' as he picked up the tinder box, tucked it into his trousers then passed me a burning stick from out of the fire: 'Take this. And always remember to take one with you whenever you travel on.'

We put out the fire and waded back to the mainland, where we shook each other's hand for the very last time: 'Good luck and God-speed my friend,' then we turned and went our separate ways.[3]

Land a short time later, and caused no further trouble for the remainder of his internment. Granted a conditional pardon in May of 1816, he returned home to his native England where he was to remain for the rest of his days.

---

[3] ***Footnote:***
George Pye never made it back to Sullivan Bay, and was presumed to have perished in the wilds of the bush.
Bill Marmon *did* make it back … suffering from scurvy but alive nonetheless. He was among the other prisoners when the settlement left for Van Diemen's Land a short time later, and caused no further trouble for the remainder of his internment. Granted a conditional pardon in May of 1816, he returned home to his native England where he was to remain for the rest of his days.

CHAPTER 4
9ᵀᴴ JANUARY, 1804

Buckley had struggled through another day without a morsel of food to sustain him, and he sat that night beneath a canopy of stars huddled up by the fire while the wild dogs howled at the moon. Lost within the memories of his childhood, he stared blankly at the trunk of a stringy-bark tree while ghostly shadows danced and swayed by the light of the flickering fire. The youngest of five children, all under the age of ten, he had been far too young to have understood just how impoverished his parents really were, and been oblivious to the fact that they had spent many sleepless nights worrying about how to make ends meet.

And when it became necessary to send him away to be raised by his grandparents, it had almost broken his heart. *"To give you a chance at a better life,"* his mother had tearfully replied when he had asked her why.

Now high up above both heaven and earth, indifferent to man and his worldly plans … an eternal sky full of endless stars looked out on this world of mice and men. And all the sad and the lonely while, he sat there alone in his prison clothes, wondering: *"Surely this cannot be the life they had wanted for me."*

Though he had lived through many solitary nights in his twenty three years, he found this night of all nights an unsettling one, for he had a sad empty feeling in the pit of his stomach, and had tossed and turned on his bed of leaves until the sun's rays emerged to drive all the shadows away. Then after taking a fire stick from out of the embers, he turned his back on the campsite and went down to the shore, where the sun was commencing its morning display ... giving off reflections of emerald green across the bay's surface in a million directions.

As he looked out across the water in the direction of the settlement, he wondered if he had done the right thing in not going back, for doubts had begun to creep into the depths of his soul as weevils will do with a barrel of flour. And he stood there thinking ... one solitary man upon this windswept coast, telling himself that what is done is done and that things will work out in the end. But his uncertainty counted for little now, for the facts were as plain as the nose on his face ... if he did not eat soon, his strength would most surely desert him.

After turning his attention to the west once more, he began heading toward a coastal headland looming in the distance like a silent sentinel sent to guard the point where the Great Southern Ocean collides with the headwaters of Port Phillip Bay. If he had wings to fly like the gulls that were gliding above his head, he would have had a bird's-eye-view of the rugged terrain running on and on for as far as the eye could see. And even if he *did* have an inkling of how difficult his task would prove to be, he could never have imagined the size of this land that he had chosen to follow ... this storm-ravaged coast stretching two thousand miles across the bottom of the continent, all the way west to the Indian Ocean.

He had been following the shore for an hour or more when his gaze happened to stray to where the sand meets up with the forest beyond. And as he strained his eyes for a closer look, he happened to notice three dogs were observing him from the margin of the trees. Having heard their howling the night before, the fact they might have now turned their attention from the moon to *he*, sent the unholiest of shivers running down his spine. And having once had the sad misfortune to have witnessed the blood-lust that a pack of wild dogs can inflict upon a flock of terrified sheep ... the thought that **he** might be seen as a target filled him with fear and trepidation. But being neither fit enough to outrun them nor strong enough to defend himself, he could see at once that his choices were few. Though he had never been one to regard himself as being any more brave than the next man, when one of the dogs locked its eyes onto his, he raised his stick and feigned to charge … yelling so loud he could have woken the dead.

And when they turned and fled like the devil himself were hot on their heels, he stood there thanking his lucky stars, so relieved to be watching them go.

He had been dragging his feet through the incessant heat, paying little heed to the surrounding terrain … a sleep-walker caught up in a monotonous rhythm of placing one foot down and then the other with nary a thought as to how or why.

And after continuing on in this trance-like state, he was brought to a halt when the beach he had been following since leaving the campsite disappeared at the base of a towering cliff. Hearing the roar of the waves as they pounded the farther side of the escarpment, he knew at once that he had arrived at the place where the bay meets up with the open sea, and he gazed up at the sandstone monolith blocking his path, wondering whether to go round the point thereby exposing himself to the force of the breakers, or avoid the waves by climbing the hill instead. He was clambering upwards a short time later when he encountered a multitude of coloured parrots chattering on a ledge some four or five yards from the top of the escarpment. He had seen many such birds since his arrival at Sullivan Bay but never in numbers as plentiful as these, and from the way in which they were squabbling up there amongst themselves, they appeared to be feeding on something that he could not see. And as he hauled himself up toward where they were gathered, they took to the air in a flap of wings … screeching their disapproval at his intrusion. When he got to the ledge, he found clusters of flowering plants growing there, many of them laden with a berry-like fruit.

And though some were ripe while others were not, he squeezed one of the ripe ones between his fingers, tasted its juice with the tip of his tongue and then helped himself to nature's bounty.

With the arrival of European white men, the plant would come to be known by the botanical name of *Corpobrotus Glaucescens* or *Pigface*,

which produces a red/purple berry-like fruit between the months of October to January and had been used as a food source by the local indigenous people for thousands of years.

After getting to his feet when he'd eaten the berries, he noticed that the glow from his fire stick had almost faded to smoke and ash, and began searching for kindling to light a fire. And as he picked up a twig a short time later, he found himself staring into the mouth of a cave. Partially hidden from view at the back of the ledge, its jagged entrance grinning a toothless grin from a craggy old face of weathered rock ... afraid at first that it might be the lair of a creature of the wild that would tear him to pieces if it knew he was there, he froze in his tracks with his heart in his mouth. Peering into the darkness until his eyes had adjusted to the shadows within ... after noting that it was nothing more than an empty cave, his fear gave way to a sigh of relief. With an opening little bigger than the width of a man's shoulders, yet large enough to permit him entry if he ducked his head, he crept inside and looked around, instantly relieved by the coolness of the air. Small in dimension ... some three or four yards in each direction, it seemed to emit both a strange and eerie aura of centuries past and a sense of serenity that he found reassuring, and having decided at once to stay there the night, he was soon sitting beside a blazing fire while ghostly shadows took to the walls to flicker and sway all around him. Both overjoyed and relieved to have found a place that could offer him protection from the burning sun, he sprawled himself out on the sandy floor and drifted off to sleep.

He left the cave a few hours later and sat on the ledge looking out to sea, hoping for a breeze that might happen along. Gazing off toward the setting sun ... he was privileged to witness the most glorious sunset there ever could be, announcing the close of day for all to see. And when *that* display was over and darkness fell, from out of the east in the opposite quarter... the giant pearl they call the moon started inching its way across the vast black canvas of twinkling stars. Overwhelmed by the grandeur of nature's display, Buckley drifted off into a conflicting patchwork of thoughts ... feeling both small and meaningless too:

"I am a mere pimple on a pumpkin that happened along, before stopping to rest for a while. And though I might dream of bigger things, the grass will still be green when I am gone."

He was reflecting upon how fate had led him to such a solitary place, when a gale blew in from out of the south, menacing clouds rolled in to blanket the stars and a thunderclap burst from out of the heavens, shaking the earth to its axis. It seemed as though angry forces were gathering in numbers planning to unleash their fury on the world around them, and in the time that it took him to get to his feet and make a dash for cover, a ferocious storm had begun pelting down upon the earth below. Buckley sat by the fire looking out from the cave as the storm raged on, wondering as he did so if Mother Nature had any more up her sleeve that could outdo the performance she had already delivered. And as he continued to dwell upon how ferocious the elements had the power to become, he glanced over at the fire … secure in the knowledge that he had more than enough firewood to last through the night. With his thoughts now dwelling upon how good fortune had led him to shelter on a night such as this, he watched on in awe as the forces of nature raged outside.

He eventually woke to see slivers of daylight creeping across the sandy floor, and after turning his attention to rekindling the fire, he went outside and climbed the few yards to the top of the escarpment. With the storm having gone and calmness restored, he was gazing off to where the cloudless sky met up in a line with the glassy sea, when his attention was drawn to a solitary seabird hovering like a hawk above the beach below. As it swooped earthwards and alighted upon a pile of kelp that had washed ashore in the storm, he watched it take flight with a fish in its beak. Aroused by the thought there might be similar opportunities awaiting *him* there, he hurried on down to investigate. What the storm had done was uproot forests of seaweed from the ocean floor and thrust them ashore with such awesome ferocity that the beach was littered with a mat of green all the way up to the high tide mark. And with the tempting vision of a wriggling fish at the front of his mind, Buckley scrambled his way down to the beach and began hungrily looking for more. Searching in vain for an hour or more, he happened to notice a clump of shellfish partly obscured under a pile of seaweed, and his heart skipped a beat at having made the discovery.

He'd found what the English refer to as mutton fish … stranded high and dry in their pearly shells, and he gleefully reached down to gather up his prize before hurrying back to the fire.

Having eaten his first real meal since God knows when, he went looking for water in the hope that the overnight rain hadn't fallen in vain, and on discovering a pool that had formed in a rocky crevice perched out of reach of the highest of tides, he settled back in the shade with his thirst now slaked, trying to keep the flies at bay. For the first time in weeks Buckley was feeling a sense of relief and with food and drink to lift his spirits, the doubts that had been plaguing him during more difficult times seemed to have drifted away with the storm. He even dared thinking of rescue again with its visions of England and home. And by the time the sun had gone down on this most favourable of days, he had amassed a pile of driftwood on the crest of the hill … just waiting to be lit at the first sign of a sail. But when a week went by with no sign of a ship, and without a further trace of food or water left for the taking, he made up his mind to move on.

It had become part of his routine to follow the shore with the position of the sun as his primary guide, and he was making his way with the wind at his back when something caught his attention off in the distance toward where he was making his way. At first he had thought it was the misty spray from the onshore breakers and had gone back to reflecting upon other things, but as he drew nearer he could see there was a river up ahead, with wisps of smoke drifting up through the trees that were lining its bank. He stopped for a moment, wondering who would be burning a fire and why, when the notion that it could be an escapee popped into his head … by chance a fellow fugitive who might be happy to welcome a kindred spirit. He then recalled having heard how sealers had come to these shores in search of prey. And if it *were* such men who had lit the fire, they may even take him on as part of their crew. But his mind then turned to more worrying things when the thought occurred that it *could* be the smoke from a native camp … perhaps even a hunting party who'd just as soon spear *him* as a kangaroo.

As he came nearer to the river and could smell the smoke, he heard the murmur of voices heading his way and then a group of blacks strode out of the woods … some ten or twelve men all carrying spears, and each one as naked as the day they were born. Stunned into silence by this white-skinned vision standing before them as tall as a tree, they stopped dead in their tracks in amazed disbelief … wondering who or what he might be. And while none of them moved as though frozen in time by a sorcerer's spell, Buckley turned on his heels and made a dash for the river before plunging straight in.

Given a different set of circumstances and a less pressing need for urgent action, he would have taken the time to note the swiftness of the current and the considerable distance to the opposite bank, and sensing the danger in entering waters as risky as these, he would have no doubt looked for a safer crossing.

But with *so* many blacks all armed to the teeth and no indication as to what their intentions might be … if he were to live to fight another day, he would need to act promptly which is just what he did. Until now, Buckley's prison clothes and his heavy boots had served him well in this rugged and oftentimes unforgiving environment, but in the hazardous waters of an outgoing tide with enough force and intensity to trouble even the strongest of swimmers, he was out of his depth to say the least. Buckley's stroke had always been sturdy and sound, his kick had always been strong, but given the odds that were stacked against him, mere swimming skills were not nearly enough … he would need more than his share of good luck as well. Though a week had passed since the violent storm that had flooded the rivers and swollen the streams, the water in which he now found himself was awash with floating debris being carried down through the waterways from higher ground. And the huge tree branch which had entered the water the night before, was being swept along in the swift-flowing current with all the momentum of a ship in full sail. With Buckley now swimming like the devil himself were driving him on, the two came together in the middle of the stream, and the branch caught his sleeve, turning him over and pulling him under … knocking the life force out of his lungs.

Had he lost his nerve and started to panic, he would have no doubt drowned right then and there. Even if his shirt had been made of a heavier weave with the strength to withstand the forces of nature being pitted against it, he would have doubtless gone to a watery grave. But the gods were feeling merciful at this moment in time and with the river about to claim its victim, his shirt sleeve tore … setting him free from the branch which held him, and he kicked and he thrust till he broke the surface coughing and gasping for air. For a moment or two, the current pulled him under for a second time … not wanting to relinquish its prize. But he refused to give in to the crippling fatigue that would have him surrender, and he struggled to fight his way back to the surface, resisting the urge to submit. With every ounce of his strength being pushed to the limit, he swam and he swam … driving himself onward with stroke after stroke, till on the verge of exhaustion and with his energy spent, his feet touched bottom on the opposite shore.

He lay on the sand gasping for air having crawled from the shallows on hands and knees, then looked back at the natives across the river … wading in the shallows with spears poised. And as he watched them catch fish after fish with relative ease … hitting a target with every attempt, he could almost smell them sizzling over a bed of hot coals. And as his mind continued to tease him thus, he was jolted back to reality when the thought hit home that in his haste to flee and get away, he had lost **his** means of lighting a fire. He almost gave up right then and there, and with a sad empty feeling in the pit of his stomach, he rolled onto his side and closed his eyes … cursing a world that would bring him to this.

The natives had gone when he came out of his stupor and got to his feet… divested himself of his waterlogged clothes before spreading them out on the sand to dry. His near-death experience had shaken him up, and the fact that he no longer had the means of lighting a fire did nothing to help his disposition. *'Perhaps I should have turned back with the others,'* he thought to himself as doubts began to creep into the forefront of his mind. But being more than six days' march away, and with the likelihood that they would have already left for Van Diemen's Land … even if he *were* to attempt it now, such an undertaking would surely end in disappointment.

He stood there gazing across the river, and as the sun began to burn his skin he headed up from the beach to the edge of the woods where the dunes gave way to the wilds of the bush. Hungry and thirsty and still a little shaky from his traumatic ordeal, he paused in the shade reflecting upon how close he had come to losing his life. There was no doubting the fact that his prospects had taken a turn for the worse with the ill-fated loss of his fire stick, and the thought of nights to come without the comfort of a fire brought on a dark cloud of despair to darken his disposition. Looking toward the river and marvelling at how accomplished the natives had been, it confirmed in his mind how ill-equipped **he** was, and how difficult it was going to be for him to cope with the hardships of this alien land. Looking down with disappointment at his cracked and weathered hands … once so useful in the life he had left behind, he knew that here so far from home, the skills of his trade were mere castles in the air. Glancing to where his prison clothes lay out on the sand in the baking heat, he wondered how long it would take before they all turned to rags in the harsh and unforgiving environment, and the mere idea of living through the depths of winter without clothes or a fire was not a thought he would choose to dwell upon. The more he reflected upon the wretched and sorry state he was in, the more dejected he became, and as he stood there feeling as if he were carrying the whole weight of the world upon his shoulders, a magpie began warbling in a nearby tree. With its poignant tune moving him almost to the point of tears, he recalled the words of his old friend Bill Marmon: *"I will always have a special place in my heart for a magpie."* Looking off in the distance toward the horizon, he wondered what Bill would have said if they had still been travelling together and smiled to himself at the thought: *'He would have no doubt found something funny to say to lighten the situation.'* Thinking of Bill told him just how much he missed him, and he hoped within his heart that they would one day meet again. He gazed off toward the west, trying to imagine what lay ahead. There was no denying the fact that his choices had dwindled since having made their escape, but he was determined in his heart to keep on going and hope that things got better.

He grew weaker and weaker as the days dragged on, and spent the past few weeks camped by a tidal creek where a two hundred yard strip of beach lay nestled in between sandstone cliffs that rose on two sides to the east and the west. He had chosen the location because he would not let go of the belief that a whaling ship or a similar vessel might happen along and take him aboard. And as the site appeared to offer a safe approach should a ship wish to anchor and put a boat ashore, he could live in hope for a little longer. He had also found a place to sleep … for under a rocky outcrop that looked out to sea from a deep depression in the sandstone cliff, he not only had protection from weather extremes, but cover on three sides should man or beast attempt to approach with the purpose of doing him harm. Having had the good fortune to discover a spring bubbling up to the surface from an underground source, apart from the fact that he now had fresh water and a place to sleep, food was getting harder and harder to come by. So desperate had he now become that the only thing he had eaten for days was a handful of shellfish and a luckless lizard that had made the mistake of crossing his path and paid the ultimate price. He had lost so much weight that his once manly frame had taken on the appearance of a raggedy scarecrow. Dishevelled and unkempt with his prison clothes hanging loose and limp from his emaciated frame, the once proud person so sturdy and strong looked more like a scrawny vagabond.

Although his long scraggly beard had the effect of limiting the sun's exposure to the peeling skin on his weather-beaten face, he was covered in bites from the hordes of mosquitoes that arrived in their thousands when the sun went down, and would only relent when it came up again. Knowing there were fish aplenty in the estuary, and having seen how successful the natives had been, he had snapped a branch from a tree and tried sharpening the end with a shard of stone. But after the fish had outwitted him time and again, he threw it away in frustration. Clinging to the belief that a ship would come and take him away … when the day finally came that he ***did*** see a sail, after watching it fade to a mere speck on the horizon, he dropped to his knees in a desperate swoon cursing a world that could be so cruel.

Compelled to face up to the harsh reality of how desperate things had now become, he dragged himself to his feet and walked away in a stupefied daze … heading off aimlessly into the bush. Everything seemed to be working against him, and he knew not how to respond. Having long grown used to following the shore, he was finding the forest a more difficult trek, as ancient trees loomed tall and imposing in every direction, while ferns and shrubs held sway over hidden gullies that ran hither and thither in the shadowy gloom. And after struggling on for the best part of an hour, the sky opened up to a sheet of blue when the forest gave way to a break in the trees, and he entered a clearing to see a human grave with a spear sticking up from the mound that contained it. Positioned at the base of a tall rock monolith standing dark and forbidding above the height of the trees, the place seemed to emit a mysterious aura that Buckley could sense but could not understand. But he approached with caution nevertheless … noting the razor-like shells embedded in resin that had hardened like stone along its murderous tip, and though he could discern on closer inspection that it was broken in two … sensing that it might prove to be useful just the same, and as *his* needs were more pressing than those of the deceased, he sought God's forgiveness by crossing himself before seizing the spear, and then left the grave to the spirit world.

Struggling on through the course of the day with fatigue dogging his progress every step of the way … wracked by hunger and with his energy flagging like never before, his poor tired legs could finally take him no further and he slumped to the ground beside a giant gum tree.

Light rain had begun to lower its misty veil when two native women happened along and saw a sleeping apparition beside a clan member's spear. And believing the mysterious spirit to be the ghost of a tribesman having returned to this earth from beyond the grave, they hurried away to relay the news.

There was another one with them upon their return … the two women along with one of their menfolk. Three shadowy figures talking in whispers, all staring in wide-eyed disbelief at the ghostly white man lying there at their feet.

CHAPTER 5
Autumn, 1804

Having surrendered myself to whatever fate may bring, I lie here feeling cold and alone, a whole world away from the place I call home and so close to death's door that I hear the voices of angels drifting on down through the misty ether, while the cold wind whistles and moans through the eucalypt trees, chilling my bones to the marrow. And as I open my eyes at the touch of a hand, I find myself eyeball to eyeball with a native tribesman, before I shift my gaze to the others beside him ... in all, three dark figures clad in animal skin cloaks, all staring at me in surprised disbelief. And when one reaches out to assist me to my feet, I accept his offer with trepidation. Now I stand before them ... most ill at ease as to what might unfold, until directed to follow by a wave of the arm, and what else could I do but obey? They led me away through the drizzling rain ... the man in the lead, the two women behind and me stumbling along in between. And after travelling thus for an hour or so with me getting weaker and weaker with each step that I took, just when I felt I could go no further, we came to a clearing where a native camp sat nestled in a gully by a trickling stream. Consisting of no more than three rustic lean-to's sitting beside the edge of the forest and a wisp of smoke drifting up to the heavens from a fire in between, in light of the miserable state I was in, it was a most pleasing sight to behold. And as two more of their kind came out to greet us … an elderly woman with a child by her side, she took one long look at the state I was in … gestured that I sit by the fire and dry myself off, and I wasted no time in complying. With the rain now gone and darkness approaching, and the glow of the fire so warm and appealing, she knelt down beside me and started raking at the embers … revealing a steaming-hot bed of leaves lying underneath the coals, seeming to serve as a blanket to keep in the heat.

A cloud of steam wafted into the air as she used a stick to lift off the leaves, and the ensuing aroma set my mouth to watering, taking me back to my grandmother's cooking when I was a lad. It smelt so good I could barely contain myself and I hung on her every move as she ladled the food into wooden bowls. I thanked my lucky stars when she filled one up and handed it to me, and when they each had a bowl and had commenced to eating, I started tucking into mine with the utmost gusto. I knew not what it was but it tasted so good I did not care … it was fresh, it was hot and that's all that mattered. And though I could not understand a single word as they chatted away amongst themselves, judging by the looks I was getting and the odd smile or two that was coming my way, there seemed little doubt that it was *I* who was the topic of conversation.

I shared a lean-to that night, and awoke at dawn to find the others preparing to vacate the camp, and in no time at all we had broken our fast and were on the move. Though I had been taught as a boy that death is the only thing certain in life, I felt sure that if their intention had been to do me harm they would have most likely done so already. So with food in my belly and a good night's sleep under my belt, I had begun to relax and observe them more closely. I was quite amazed at how they were able to move in such a way that their bare feet made hardly a sound. Whereas with my big heavy boots and my clumsy ways, *I* would be making enough noise to awaken the dead. But they continued on nevertheless, pausing but once for a brief repast and a call to nature, and when they finally came to a halt on the crest of a hill, we were able to view the terrain for miles around. They were pointing to a village off in the distance positioned close by to a shimmering lake, and judging by the way they were talking as they gazed in its direction, they seemed to have answered my thoughts as to where we were headed, and though I must confess to feeling apprehensive as to what might lay ahead, I had no choice but to follow. Having covered the rest of the journey in no time at all, we were soon passing by huts to the left and huts to the right as word of our arrival seemed to have raced on ahead, until a crowd of natives had gathered around us, and we were caught in the midst of a bustling throng and able to proceed not one step further.

It was plain to see that *I* was the one who was attracting the attention as a crowd of natives, mainly women and children were all jostling to get close enough to look me over. The entire assemblage were staring and gawking as though I were a two-headed freak being touched and pawed by all and sundry. It felt like I had fallen from the sky into an alien world, and as I stood there wondering what to do, a hush came over the gathering as they all moved aside to allow a man to approach me from the back of the crowd. You could have heard a pin drop as he stopped in front of me and looked me straight in the eye. He was at least a foot shorter than I, but judging by the way in which everyone had gone so deathly quiet, he appeared to be a man of considerable importance. Totally naked from head to toe with a bone inserted through the septum of his nose, he had a full beard peppered with streaks of grey. He appeared to be some twenty-odd years my senior, with only one eye and a hideous scar marking the place where the other had been. And when that one eye fixed me with a spine-tingling stare, I felt a shiver of fear run right through me which I tried my best to conceal. I had come across more than my share of fearsome fighting men in my military days, but none more so than this man now before me. Though he carried no weapon that I was able to see, I had the distinct feeling that he could have struck me down dead if he had chosen to do so. There was not a sound to disturb the scene until I heard the lonely cry of a mournful crow, and as the solitary bird left its branch and took to the air, the one-eyed man raised his head and sniffed the air … started moving his lips as though casting a spell upon the clouds in the sky, and after shifting his gaze to my broken spear, he placed a hand upon my shoulder then turned and walked away. I stood transfixed … wondering what I might be in for next as the others began crowding around me once again. Some started tearing out clumps of their hair … moaning and making sorrowful lamentations as though grieving the loss of a dying child. Confused, bewildered, all at sixes and sevens … my emotions were pulling me this way and that until a woman came toward me from out of the crowd and they all moved aside to allow her approach. Whoever she was, she wasted no time in taking my hand to lead me away to one of the huts.

She gave me food, she gave me water, she smiled a smile so warm and tender that quickly put me at my ease, and having been freed for the moment from the madness outside, I took a deep breath to gather my thoughts. Too tall for the hut, I sat down by the fire at her behest and glanced around her living space while she turned her attention to other things. Built of bigger dimensions and of more permanent means than the lean-to in which I had spent the night, it looked to be large enough to sleep three people or perhaps four at a pinch, with the coals in the fire glowing warm and appealing in a shallow recession in the earthen floor while its smoke drifted up through a gap in the sticks and the brush that served as a roof. She had a number of items lying off to one side ... dilly bags, wooden vessels for food and drink and an odd assortment of implements of varying shapes and sizes. Next to them lay weapons of war ... spears and other instruments specifically made for hunting and killing, all looking lethal in every respect. From what I was able to tell, each and every item appeared to have been made with craftsmanship and an eye for detail, and as I cast my eye around the rest of the hut, I counted beds numbering three ... two side by side with a smaller one positioned just a few feet away, with each one consisting of animal skin rugs spread over mattresses made of reeds and rushes. As I turned my attention back to the lady, I noticed her making up a fourth one on the other side of the hut and sat watching her while she did so. I took a guess at her age, reckoning it to be close to that of my mother ... some two score years with a little to spare, and as she finished her task and got to her feet, a little boy came through the doorway and rushed to her side. He clasped his arms around her waist, gave me a wary look as though I might be the devil himself come to take him away, and when I gave him a smile, he shyly responded with one of his own. I saw him whisper in her ear, and upon seemingly getting a reply he approved of, he dashed back out through the doorway with a grin on his face. No sooner had he gone when I heard the sound of voices raised, and as the woman got to her feet and beckoned me to follow, she led the way outside and into the open where some two dozen tribesmen had arrived at the camp, with the entire village having come out to greet them.

Even their dogs joined in the occasion ... barking as though each and every one of them knew there was food for the taking and were determined not to miss out.

They appeared to be men from the village just returned from a hunt, having killed a big red kangaroo and two smaller ones that were grey in colour, and on seeing me standing in the middle of the crowd, they turned their attention from the catch to me. Once again I became the topic of discussion as my presence was explained by one of the women, and when she had satisfied the others that all was well, the crowd's focus quickly turned back to the catch. Judging by the number of smiles flashing pearly-white teeth in every direction, the hunt had been a huge success, and in no time at all the animals were being skinned and dissected and shared out amongst all those present. Now free of the confusion I had previously been feeling, I began observing the villagers a little more closely... noting that many of the women were adorned with netted head bands, and necklaces strung with pieces of shell. Some even had a bird's feather attached there as well. A few had ornamental bones stuck through their noses, but smaller and more refined than the one being worn by the one-eyed man. As far as the menfolk were concerned: they appeared to be in general lithe and athletic, with most wearing loin cloths or nothing at all. Like the one-eyed man, some had a bone inserted through the septum of their nose, perhaps as a token of manhood I was inclined to think, or even a symbol of their warrior status. Whatever the case, following their skilful execution of the job at hand they had shared out the meat in no time at all. Then as the crowd began dispersing and drifting away, the mysterious lady reappeared and took me once more to her hut. This time the one-eyed man was seated in the place where I sat before, and directed me to sit as he saw me enter. As I did as requested, he turned his attention back to what he'd been doing ... wrapping up some meat in a parcel of leaves, and upon completing that task while I sat there watching, he covered it over with a blanket of coals. Reaching then for what appeared to be a short-handled axe, he started honing the blade with a sharpening stone ... working and working its lethal edge until the boy rushed back into the hut, gave them both a kiss and a hug before turning his attention to things of his own.

There was no doubting the fact that they were a family unit... husband and wife if I were to hazard a guess. And the boy? ... perhaps their son or their grandson, and by the look of the four food bowls she'd laid out on a mat and the extra bed that she had gone to the trouble of preparing, I was beginning to get the feeling they were planning to take me in as one of their own. Whatever the case, being in no position to pick and choose, I made up my mind to make the best of the situation come what may.

When I sat with them later sharing their meal, she attempted to teach me some of their language. She called me **Murrungurk** ... pointing to me as she repeated the name until I caught onto her meaning, and when I said it myself, the boy giggled and giggled as I did so. As she introduced the boy as **Trawalla,** there were smiles all round when I got that right too. She called herself **Connewarre**, and I received nods of approval when I managed that as well. That only left the one-eyed man. His name was **Darn-Garreeyn-Waa,** and though I did my best to get it right, I found the name well-nigh impossible to get my tongue around.

They had gone to great lengths to make me feel welcome, and with sheer determination and a whole lot of patience, she more or less managed the task of making herself understood. Then as the afternoon rolled on and my hosts had gone off to attend to business, I heard the hustle and bustle of comings and goings outside the hut so I went outside to see what was happening. With the sun about to drop below the tree line and the villagers scurrying hither and thither as though something important were about to occur, *my* attention turned to other things ... for as I felt the need come upon me for a call to nature, I headed off to spend some time on my own. I had squatted beside a tree a few minutes later, only to look up and notice that the one-eyed man was perched up in a tree some twenty yards or so from where I was sitting. Although that was a weird enough thing in itself, as I strained my eyes for a closer look, I saw a bird sitting up there on the branch beside him. It looked like a crow in every sense of the word but was as white as white could possibly be, and with things becoming more and more mysterious with every second that passed, as my eyes adjusted to the fading light I could see that he and the bird were staring right at me.

It goes without saying how uneasy I felt at the embarrassing position that I found myself in as I finished the task just as fast as I could, and as I looked up again after getting to my feet to pull up my trousers ... there was not a trace of man or bird anywhere to be seen. I had always regarded myself as a more than capable climber when I was a boy, but upon looking more closely at the tree in question ... there was not *one* single branch between where he'd been sitting and the ground below, and not a chance in hell I could ever have climbed it. Then there was the matter of the mysterious bird ... had it been a figment of my imagination? I could think of no explanation that made any sense as I hurried on back to the village. With night having fallen by the time I got back, the place was abuzz with excitement with a bonfire blazing and a crowd having gathered while seating themselves around its perimeter. The next thing I knew, the boy Trawalla was standing beside me and after placing his little hand in mine, he led me over to sit down among them. Then the women came out of their huts ... each and every one carrying fur skin cloaks, and apart from the occasional head band or necklace ... all were as naked as the day they were born. I noted my hostess among them as they seated themselves in front of the fire with their backs to those of us sitting behind and as I sat there wondering what was about to unfold, a dozen ghost-like men sprung out of the darkness, all of them daubed with chalky white paint streaked in thin broken lines along their black spindly arms and their spidery legs ... a more phantasmagorical group of creatures I could never have imagined.

No sooner had they come into the firelight when the click click clicking of sticks upon sticks started tapping in time with the beating of drums. Sitting cross-legged with their cloaks stretched tightly across their knees, the women began beating their makeshift drums with the palms of their hands ... thump thump thumping in rhythm with the clicking of sticks, and as the sounds grew louder and the night seemed to offer its sanction by beating along with the pulsating tempo, a man's voice rang out in a nasally chant ... singing an eerie incantation over and over while the ghostly figures began performing their dance. I watched in awe as they stamped their feet in stick-figure-like movements while the magical performance slowly unfolded right there before me.

Every gesture seemed to be a lively enactment of some macabre ritual, and I sat there transfixed, caught up in the mystery of something rare and unique ... thump, thump, thump, thump ... tap, tap, tap, tap ... each note delivered in perfect time with the man's trancelike voice, while the stars shone down in twinkling approval, and the glow of the fire and the dust and the smoke sent a powdery mist drifting into the night as the performers eyes glowed with a white-hot passion like the fires that explode from the vaults of hell.

They danced and they danced on into the night, with all eyes fixed upon every step of their performance as though life and death hung in the balance and could tip either way at a moment's notice. Swept up as I was in the extravaganza, I was carried along on a magical journey into a world far beyond one I could ever have imagined. And though I had no idea how long it had lasted ... for I had lost all sense of time and space, by the time a cheer rang out followed by two more of the same in quick succession, the spell was broken just as quickly as it started.

The fire had died down to an amber glow as the night crept back in like the incoming tide to reclaim control of its nocturnal domain, and as the crowd began stirring and drifting away, I noticed the boy was asleep with his head in my lap. I sat for a moment, reflecting upon the innocence of one so small ... pondering how quickly it changes as we all have to face life's difficult trials, then after looking up to see that his mother was awaiting us outside the hut, I carried him over to her waiting arms.

It had been a night like no other, and sleep managed to elude me until the wee small hours finally wore me down and into submission, and the next thing I knew ... the grey misty veil of another new dawn was peeking through the doorway into the hut. Rising to find they had left food out by the foot of my bed, I went outside after breaking my fast where for the third day in a row, the sky wore a blanket of steely grey and the cold winds were sending an ominous warning that winter was coming and would not be kept waiting. I looked down at my worn out clothes ... wondering how long it would be before they gave up the ghost and fell off my back and I pondered as to how I would cope when that day came.

But I put such thoughts to the back of my mind ... determined to take things one day at a time. Looking around me, I happened to notice that some of the villagers were gathered around down by the lake, so I wandered on down to join them. As I walked down the hill, I noticed the terrain was awash with a carpet of daisies, with a number of women and children kneeling down digging them out of the ground. I had seen many of these wildflowers of late, but until this moment I had not known that these bright yellow flowers had edible tubers ... the kind we ate with our meal just one day before. As I passed on by, I could see the waterway spread out before me at closer range ... noting how substantial it was from way up here on the higher ground. I could also see that it was connected to the sea by a reed-fringed channel and what appeared to be the very same estuary in which I had almost drowned just a few days before. And there was the familiar face of Connewarre wading with the others up to their knees, and having noticed my approach, she bid that I join them with a wave of the arm. There were some twenty-odd villagers ...

men women and children, spread out at a distance of some two hundred yards, wading along by the edge of the lagoon. In spite of the chilly conditions, their cloaks all lay in a pile by the water's edge with most being naked now as a result. As I drew nearer I could see some were wearing string-like fabric tied around their waists with dilly bags to hold what it was they were collecting, and as I felt disinclined to offend or displease ... in spite of the fact that the water was cold, I took off my boots, rolled up my trousers and waded on in to join them. Whatever it was they were occupied with, they seemed to be having a really good time, and as Trawalla came over to take hold of my hand, he led me over to one of the men. I recognised him as one of the performers from the night before, but in the cold light of day without the blazing fire and the thrill of the occasion, he was just another face in the crowd. I soon found out they were all feeling for molluscs with their feet and their toes, and putting them in the bags that hung from their waists, and as the boy and I went to lend a hand, we helped fill up a bag in no time at all.

We used to call them cockles back home in England, but these were a whole lot bigger and looked far more appetising than any others I'd seen, and I could hardly wait for the feast to begin.

Later in the day I had wandered off for some time on my own, and happened upon an ancient tree of gigantic proportions that had been severely damaged by a lightning strike. With an enormous gash in the middle of its trunk that opened up into a charred and blackened cavity as big as a cave, what remained of this once-mighty giant was now so weathered and bleached by the effects of the sun that it looked as if it had been dead for a long long time. I took a look inside and saw that someone had fitted it out with a rough form of shelving ... seemingly to use as a smoking room for the preserving of food, and the accumulation of ash that covered its floor seemed to confirm that this might be the case. Taking a step back to gaze up into what was left of its canopy, I tried to imagine how it would have looked when in its prime ... musing as I did so on how the ravages of time spare nothing or no one, no matter how big or no matter how small, and as I continued to reflect upon how time catches up with us all in the end, I noticed that the sun was dropping below the horizon so I headed on back before it got dark. Once again the place was a hive of activity upon my return, with some of the villagers making things out of what appeared to be reeds from the lake, so I stopped to observe what it was they were doing. They were threading one piece over then the next one under as one would do when weaving a basket and as they noticed me watching, I was handed one for a closer look. It was circular in shape, light in weight, and being turned up as it was around the rim ... I assumed it was a basket for the serving food, and having made a dozen or so in no time at all, they got to their feet and went over to where a fishing net lay folded up beside one of the huts and when I saw how they were struggling to pick it up, I went over to give them a hand. It was unlike any net that I had ever seen ... seeming to have been made from a type of flax. Although it looked a little rough and somewhat fibrous and bulky ... judging by the *other* things I had seen that they'd made, I was sure it had been fashioned with both skill and precision.

Whatever the case ... it seemed we were about to test it out, for as we proceeded to carry it on down the hill, the whole village was coming along to be a part of the occasion. Some were carrying bundles of firewood, with others in charge of the baskets, while the rest had fire sticks lighting our way. It was beginning to look like another big event was about to unfold, with even the moon peeping out from behind a cloud ... watching our progress every step of the way ... determined to not miss a thing. As I followed their lead when they took off their coats by the water's edge, those with the baskets set them to floating on top of the water ... seemingly checking to ensure none of them sank. Then they placed handfuls of wet sand into each basket followed by firewood too on top of the sand, and when that job was done, we were given the cue to haul the net out into the lake. It had all happened so fast that the water was up to our chest in no time at all, and by the time one of them gave us the signal to stop, I looked back in the direction of those on the beach and saw a dozen tiny fires flickering out there through the darkness, burning in a line as they bobbed along in the shallows like floating lanterns shining their light out across the water. As we started dragging the net back to shore ... drawing nearer and nearer to the glow of the fires, the water began to bubble and foam with fish darting hither and thither in a state of confusion, for having been lured to the lights like moths to a flame, they were caught in a trap with no means of escape. With the net getting heavier and heavier with every step that we took, it was soon so full that we could drag it no further. That was the point where those on the beach rushed into the water to give us a hand ... heaving and hauling as hard as we could until we managed to drag it up onto the beach. As I watched the net spill out onto the sand ... that's when I saw they weren't fish after all, but a squirming mass of wriggling eels. The level of excitement had reached fever-pitch with the desperate creatures glistening and shining like flashes of silver in the misty moonlight... flipping and flopping all over the place, with every man woman and child clubbing and spearing with reckless abandon until every last one had been put to the sword. Then following a momentary pause in proceedings ... just as I was thinking of a place by the fire, they took me straight back out there to do it all again.

I was chilled to the bone by the time we carried the net back up to the village, and when we had eaten our fill at the feast that followed, the massive surplus of eels was taken away to be smoked and cured for the days ahead. It had been yet another example of how adept they were at making the most of the opportunities that came their way, and I was greatly impressed at what I had seen. Moreover, as well as the skills I had seen them displaying at every turn, they seemed to get along with each other so very well that I had not heard an angry word uttered since my arrival. At least that had been my initial impression, but when an incident occurred just a few days later, I had to rethink that opinion.

It involved the man they called Jillong .... the one we had helped to gather the cockles, and whom I had since come to learn was the youngest son of the one-eyed man. I of course would have been able to make more sense of what I was about to witness if I had even a basic understanding of some of their language, but as I did not, I had to try reading between the lines as the situation unfolded before my eyes, and I will endeavour to give my version of what occurred: I had been awoken at sunrise by angry voices, and after peeking out of my doorway to see what was happening, I saw two men standing outside Jillong's hut. Due to the fact that they were armed with spears and seemingly challenging him to come outside, it appeared that there might be trouble afoot. When he *did* come out a moment later ... he not only had a small-handled axe in his hand, but had a young woman standing beside him as well. Though I was to find out later that she was his new young bride ... in spite of the fact that they began addressing their concerns directly to *him*, I could not help getting the impression that their conversation was more about her. And as their discussions continued and the tension mounted to such an extent that a violent outcome was seeming inevitable, the one-eyed man come out of his hut. He stood perfectly still ... his steely gaze moving from one to the other, and as he started addressing them, his calm easy manner seemed to be having the immediate effect of defusing what that had seconds before seemed like a powder keg about to explode. And as it began to appear as though their grievances had been resolved when he reached the point where there was no more to say, Jillong and his wife had turned to go.

I was about to do the same when one of the strangers let out a spine-tingling yell and the next thing I knew, the girl had been hit in the shoulder by the assailant's spear. In the blink of an eye the one-eyed man had him by the throat … strangling the life-force out of his body, and as the second man leapt to the other's defence, he was struck dead on the spot by a blow from the axe. My head was spinning from what I had witnessed, and as Jillong rushed to her aid and carried her back to her hut, I turned back to *my* hut to try to make sense of what I had seen. With two men dead and a young girl injured, although it might be said that the issue had been settled and what's done is done … if it had been due to some kind of feud or an affair of the heart as it seemed to have been, I doubt if we had heard the last of it.

Several days later a messenger arrived at the village, and with Trawalla on hand to try to explain to me what was occurring, I picked up the fact that the man had been sent to invite our people to come and visit his clan. Drawing my attention to the four red lines that had been painted across the man's forearm, the boy pointed a finger toward the east, before sweeping an arc across the sky until his arm was pointing west. I assumed he was trying to tell me that each red mark signified one day's travel from the place where the man had started out, and if that were the case and I was reading him correctly … for him to have embarked on such a lengthy journey, the man's mission must have been of the utmost importance. The boy then explained how the discussions were concerning a proposed trading of goods between the visitor's tribe and ours, and when the man passed his axe around for the group to inspect, he seemed to be offering the tool as a part of the deal. Though I knew it not at the time, I would come to learn that the stone they used in making their axes was both highly prized and hard to come by, and the place where the visitor's tribe happened to reside was one of the very few sites where it could be found in apparent abundance. As one of our people came forward and handed the visitor one of our eels, it appeared they were considering swapping some of our eels for some of their stone. They passed around refreshment while the talks continued and there were smiles all round when they reached an agreement.

I knew it not at the time, but a part of their agreement would involve most of our people packing up their belongings to accompany the messenger back to his village. Nor was I aware that tribes *often* broke into smaller family groups before leaving an area when resources became scarce. And with winter on the way and the available food sources about to decline, the people seemed to have an innate sense to be able to gauge how long to stay, and know the best time to leave. They staged another dance performance on that final night, and although most of them set off the following morning, it seemed our group was to remain until Jillong's wife had recovered and was able to travel. That was when I learned she was expecting a child, and when we *did* finally leave some two weeks later, instead of following where the others had gone, we went off instead in the opposite direction. Now that we were on the move, I kept to the rear and out of the way, being painfully aware that my clumsy presence was a constant liability to those up ahead. I had finally come to the realisation that to survive in the wild, one had to be on one's guard and alert at all times. In *their* case however, such an awareness seemed to come as second nature, and every minute that I was to spend in their company would further confirm just how skilful they were at observing even the smallest of things: A tiny scuff mark for example would have them stop dead in their tracks and study it closely before moving on.

Even something as seemingly insignificant as a broken twig would not go unnoticed. And an almost undetectable animal print would have them freeze on the spot and sniff the air, listening for any tell-tale sounds that could mean the difference between life and death. As for me … I had a lot to learn but was eager to do so. As the morning rolled by into afternoon, we were heading in the direction of a mountain range looming taller and taller the closer we got, and within an hour or so we had begun climbing a narrow path, hugging a wall of sheer granite that was covered in moss and evergreen ferns clinging for dear life to the cracks and the crevices that had become their home. As the peaks rose higher and higher before disappearing far above us in the swirling mist, cold mountain water trickled on down over the rock face then spilled over the cliff to the forest far below.

The cool misty air created the illusion we were walking through a rain cloud drifting high above the earth, while the view across the landscape had me yearn to linger longer, if only they would pause so I could stop and take it in. But we pushed on regardless, and by the time we'd crossed over the summit and were on our way down ... with nightfall closing in to restrict further progress, we came to a halt where the track opened out onto what appeared to be a ledge suspended there like a saviour hard up against the side of the mountain. I stood there for a moment surveying the scene. Although it was little more than three or four yards from one side to the other, it appeared to be as good a place as any for us to stop and spend the night. It was certainly a far safer alternative than continuing down that narrow trail with no light to guide us. Be that as it may, I was also conscious of the fact that little more than three or four yards across to my right ... the ledge fell away and became a sheer drop that plunged hundreds of feet to the forest below. Nevertheless, they set about gathering what little firewood there was to be had, and we soon had a crackling fire burning. All we could find for a lean-to however were a couple of dozen fern fronds and very little else. But in spite of all that, we had settled down around the fire trying to make the most of a difficult situation, when a flash of lightning and a clap of thunder sounded a warning of what the night would have in store. I have never been one to be afraid of the dark, but I was beginning to feel an eerie nervousness that I could not explain, and was ever-so glad to be in the company of friendly faces. Nightfall came upon us with an almighty rush, and there was not one single star to wish upon. Even the moon seemed reluctant to show itself, choosing instead to hide stealthily away like a thief in the night. So we huddled up together around what there was of a fire ... six solitary figures from two different worlds. And when the drizzle turned to rain and quickly got the better of the sputtering flames, we all made a dash for the lean-to ... each to have to cope with what the night might choose to bring.

The sun rose slowly ... sluggishly even, seemingly too lazy to let the day get underway, and I opened my eyes and saw that the others were up and preparing to get underway.

As I dragged my weary bones out from our soggy bed of leaves, every fibre of my being was expressing displeasure at what had been inflicted upon it, and though my poor empty stomach was already feeling like my throat had been cut, I got to my feet in spite of all that and we were back on our way with not a moment's delay. Now that the sun was breaking through to lift our spirits, I was musing over what the day might bring, when from out of nowhere it seemed as if every feathered creature for miles around had taken it upon themselves to celebrate the fact that a whole new day was presenting itself.

And as more and more joined in the chorus the further we descended … the more visible the countryside was in fact becoming. It was already beginning to reveal a vast panorama of verdant green for miles and miles in every direction. And while everything was getting bigger and bigger the closer we got, all at once the trail curved around to our left near the bottom of the hill and showed an entirely different vista for all to see.

I paused briefly to gaze off to the horizon where I was able to discern the blue-grey colour of a distant lake. It looked as if a shimmering mirage had been placed out there to show us the way, and when someone up ahead pointed a finger in that direction and a few words were murmured from one to the other, we continued to travel onward in the lake's direction. And after several more minutes of journeying, we were brought to a halt by the one-eyed man. He and Jillong had got down on their knees … whispering to each other as they peered into an animal burrow that had been dug into the side of a sandy embankment. I had seen many fox lairs and rabbit burrows back home in England, but never had I seen one as big as this. And as I stood there watching for what they'd do next, they got up off their knees … whispered a few quiet words to each other, then picked up their spears and we were back on our way. We continued to travel thus for an hour or so until we got to the lake and could proceed no further. We were also standing in the midst of what would have once been a copse of eucalyptus trees, but they were now all bleached to a ghostly grey and were long-since dead. Gazing about me in every direction, I saw a dozen or so weather-beaten lean-tos as well, but judging by the tumbled-down state they were in, they appeared to have been abandoned a long time ago.

As I stood there trying to take it all in, Connewarre went over to one of the trees and started giving it a tap with her old wooden club. She had my attention I will grant you that, and after putting her ear up against the tree and pausing to listen, she moved on to another one before repeating the process. Then as her face lit up with a toothy smile, she called us over to see what she'd found. Stripping off a piece of bark … she revealed to the daylight a seething mass of insects swarming all over its rotted-out trunk. I took a step forward for a closer look, thinking at first that they might have been termites. But a closer inspection showed them to be a whole lot bigger, more like a cricket in size and shape. Much laughter and merriment broke out amongst the gathering, and when Connewarre picked one up and put it in her mouth …

savouring it like it was a mouth-watering delicacy, the others were quick to do likewise. Then to my dismay, Trawalla picked one up and handed it to me, grinning from ear to ear as he did so. My first inclination was to follow my instincts and decline the offer, but I remembered my manners and held out my hand and nodded my head, although I did so with much trepidation. It was not at all bad to the taste … in fact I am the first one to admit that I was pleasantly surprised, and I was just about to try another when Jillong and his father picked up their spears and a coil of rope and called both the boy and myself to follow. We headed back in the same direction from where we'd just come, and as near as I was able to hazard a guess, we were seemingly going back to the burrow. Whether I was right or whether I was wrong, Trawalla was jumping out of his skin with excited expectation. And when my guess was confirmed a short time later, the one-eyed man tied the rope around the boy's wrist … whispering words of encouragement as he did so. Then I was handed the rope and could do nothing more than look on in horror, as the boy got down on his knees before wriggling backwards down into the hole. As I watched him disappear out of sight, the rope suddenly took on a whole different meaning … perhaps it was even the boy's only link between life and death. And while it passed ever-so-slowly through my trembling hands, Jillong and his father jumped up onto the embankment and knelt down on all-fours, both with an ear to the ground.

I felt like a fish out of water, looking on helplessly as I was, while the other two went about their business … pausing to listen before crawling a little further then stopping again. I have to admit that I was having grave doubts about the wisdom of such a dubious enterprise, for as they crawled further and further away from the hole, I was getting an indication of just how big the tunnel was proving to be. And with the coil of rope getting smaller and smaller in my quivering hands, to my relief, Jillong finally gave me the signal to start retrieving it in just a little at a time. Although I was unable to see him, I could feel him edging his way back to me ever so slowly, as I knelt there ever so nervously with my heart in my mouth. And after several more minutes that felt like hours … I saw his dusty little hands come into the light, then his forearms appeared, and when his head and his shoulders followed a second or two later, I looked to the heavens and thanked the Lord. Now that he was up on his feet like a jack-in-the-box, with me dusting him down while he stood there grinning like a Cheshire cat, the others got straight down to the business of digging the creature out of its lair. We took it in turns at the task of digging the hole and it took us an age I can assure you of that, but after we finally broke through and could now see its lair … several more minutes of digging followed by three or four thrusts of Jillong's hunting spear, and the creature had been dispatched to kingdom come. It took a group effort for us to haul its dead weight up out of the hole, where we could now see more clearly just how big it was. It only served to confirm that things could so easily have had a far less favourable outcome. It was almost as big as the boy himself, and by the look of its powerful claws and its razor-like teeth, I imagine it could have put up one hell of a fight if cornered and had chosen to mount an attack. While I stood there staring, Jillong curled its lip back to show us its teeth… revealing one long razor-sharp incisor on either side of both its upper and lower jaw. Trawalla reached down to test one for sharpness, as his *own* pearly-white teeth lit up with another proud grin. Carrying it all the way back to camp was far from easy, but the end result certainly justified the means. And now that it was getting on toward the end of the day, while the tantalising aroma of the creature baking in its bed of hot coals was tempting our senses, we joined with the women at gathering termites.

They were even tastier when roasted over the coals on a sheet of bark, and with so much fresh meat to sustain us, along with our seemingly inexhaustible supply of edible termites, we spent quite a few contented days in that most bountiful place. But just when I started lulling myself into thinking that the times of plenty might go on forever, we had gone to the trees to gather more termites, only to find they had all disappeared, leaving nothing but hundreds upon hundreds of empty husks … the only visible evidence they'd even been there at all.

CHAPTER 6

Another two seasons of freedom

By the time winter arrived with its turbulent winds that blew cold and unforgiving, it was the beginning of my third change of season since having made my escape. The blistering summer that had brought heat and dry winds beyond anything I could ever have imagined had been followed by an autumn that tempered the land. With my hair now down past my shoulders and my long scruffy beard … I doubt if my own mother would have recognised me if she had happened along. And though my trusty old boots were doing their best to keep serving my needs, I had discarded my prison clothes for the opossum coat that Connewarre had given me when she welcomed me into her family circle. We had abandoned the termite site some weeks before and had moved two days' travel further inland and settled in a wooded valley beside a mountain stream … just the sort of watercourse that the poets might refer to as a babbling brook. Apart from it being a pleasure to look upon, the place also offered a degree of protection from inclement weather where we could position our lean-tos close to the rocky crags and giant boulders which dominate the hills and the fern gullies and gave us a degree of shelter from even the severest of cold winter gusts. There is an enormous hollow tree there as well, which when I stepped inside was larger than the cottage in which I had spent my youth. And there's a waterfall a little further upstream ... its crystal clear waters tumbling down over black granite boulders to churn up this section of the river into white water rapids seemingly determined to race to the coast as though the waiting ocean had somewhere to go and was in too much of a hurry to wait any longer. And In spite of the fact that I came from a different world, I was feeling a sense of belonging and likened the valley to a Garden of Eden, and if I dare say it ... I felt a little like Adam without his Eve.

With Trawalla in the role of my trusty tutor, I was slowly acquiring an understanding of their peculiar language, with him delighting in teaching me more of their ways. Game was harder to come by now that winter was upon us, but with the men's hunting skills and this most bounteous valley they had brought us to, we were usually assured of food for the table in *spite* of the difficult season. There were many times when the men would be off hunting for days on end, and with the women usually busying themselves with a variety of chores, Trawalla and I took every opportunity to practise our *own* hunting techniques whenever we could. On one such occasion we had followed the river further upstream and stumbled upon a giant lizard stretched out upon a rock, seemingly making the most of what little sunshine happened to be filtering through to the forest floor. It was at least four feet long from its head to its tail, and upon seeing two strange predators had happened along and disturbed its slumber, it tried to make a dash for the nearest tree. As quick as a flash, the boy was after it ... delivering a deathly whack with his club as it attempted to scuttle its way off up the trunk, and as it dropped back to earth and tried crawling away into the scrub, it was stopped dead in its tracks by another swift clout that finished the job in no uncertain terms. Needless to say when it was cooked over the coals a few hours later, it provided us all with a most tasty feast.

By now Jillong's wife was heavy with child ... with an air of expectation pervading the camp, and no lack of pampering or shortage of attention from the father-to-be, and long may good fortune shine upon the both of them I hasten to say. Along with the other vegetation that flourished throughout the valley, there was a species of tree that grew in strands in some parts of the forest. Although hard to find, the men put a lot of effort into seeking it out and whenever they managed to locate some, they would give the stems the same knock and tap test that Connewarre had done with the hollow trees when she'd been searching for termites. Then upon finding a stem that sounded hollow, they would chop it down ... scour out the wood that was left inside, then cut it into two-foot lengths about the thickness of my arm.

After blocking off one end and inserting a piece of netting into the other, they glued the netting in place so it formed a funnel at the cylinder's entrance.

Then after putting some rotten meat or a fish head inside, they positioned it somewhere along the river and attached it to something to prevent it from moving. The idea was to lure an eel or a yabby into the trap, and while the ingenious funnel allowed the quarry to enter the cylinder in search of the bait, it prevented it from leaving when it tried to escape. The boy and I positioned a number of these in various locations along the river, and I never ceased to feel a sense of excited anticipation whenever we returned to see what we'd caught. On another one of our hunting excursions, Trawalla had stopped beside a huge hollow tree ... seeming to momentarily sniff its trunk before calling me over to point something out. I saw nothing of interest at my first attempt, but after he insisted I take a closer look, I noticed a tiny tuft of hair caught in its bark. Smiling a self-satisfied smile as he handed me his club, he started climbing the tree as though born to the task, and within a matter of minutes he'd dragged an opossum out of its hole and sent it hurtling down to the ground below. Needless to say I kept my part of the bargain with a blow from the club and the boy scrambled back down with all the tree-climbing skill of a chimpanzee, before we proudly carried it back to the camp. These were the happiest of times to be sure, to be sure ... days that I would look back upon with joyful fondness for many a long year. But when childbirth arrived on a cold winter's night ... without the happy accompaniment of an infant's cry, the still-born child was lain to rest in a grave when the sun came up to mark the new day. Several days later as the first rays of sunshine peeped through the trees ... on having noticed the fire was about to go out, I went off on my own to gather some firewood. The morning dew had covered the ground with a blanket of silver, and while the river was bathed in a ghostly mist, I stopped to watch a wading bird standing in the shallows as still as a statue on the lookout for prey. As it started to probe the mud with its sabre-like beak, another bird in a nearby tree let out a raucous cackle... seemingly trying to let the whole world know it could see humour in everything both great and small, and those that did not could please themselves.

The gentle flow of this part of the stream seemed to amble along as though it had nowhere to go and all the time in the world to get there, and while I felt the cold coming up through the now paper-thin soles of my trusty old boots … in spite of the chilly conditions warning me against it, I was so much in need of a wash that I stripped off my clothes and waded on in to bathe in the shallows. Needless to say, the icy waters led to my decision not to linger too long, and I was drying myself off a short time later when I happened to look up into a tree for no other reason than purely by chance, and surprise of all surprises … another white crow was perched up in a branch there staring at me. I had no way of knowing whether it was the same bird as last time, but whether it was or whether it was not …

I wasted no time in tarrying there. I was on my way back to camp a short time later with an armful of firewood, when I saw Jillong's wife sitting by a bend in the river, gazing across the water with a look of despair that would have melted the coldest of hearts. Seemingly oblivious to the fact that I was anywhere near, at the risk of intruding on her moment of grief, I chose to pass by in silence and left the poor girl to mourn on her own.

We were managing to survive the cold days of winter better than I could ever have imagined, and as the weather got warmer while the days rolled by, we were still camped beside the river by the time spring finally arrived to drive away the cold. And with the birds now heralding in the new season of growth, we finally broke camp and returned to the place where the edible termites had provided us all with so much bounty. The fields were now covered with splashes of yellow from yam daisy flowers colouring the terrain in every direction, and there were bees in their thousands trying to pay a visit to each and every one. With the lake having taken on a life of its own, all manner of water birds were flocking to the water to breed among the reeds with their mating calls growing to such a cacophony of sounds that it seemed as if every feathered creature on the face of the earth had flown in to celebrate the arrival of spring, with the whole damn lot of them wanting to join in the party.

On the day we arrived, more of our clan members came to join us, swelling our numbers to some forty-odd strong, and it quickly became apparent that their reason for coming was because the lake had an island where birds came to nest. And as the waters of the lake were relatively shallow, it was a simple matter to wade out there and gather their eggs. In addition to that, the men had a clever way of catching the birds. One of them would cut a length of hollow reed ... submerge himself underwater and by using the reed to enable him to breathe, he approached any unwary bird that was oblivious to the fact that danger was near, and when he was close enough to reach its legs, he dragged it under and wrung its neck. There were other advantages to our location as well, for with such vast amounts of yam daisy flowers growing nearby, the trees had become home to so many bees that there was every indication we would have a supply of honey for some time to come. By now I had come to learn that hunting was a role undertaken by the men, and with their knowledge of the tides and the phases of the moon, they were able to determine when the best time was for catching fish, and invited me along on one such occasion. There were a dozen of us in all ... each man armed with a spear and spread out at a distance of ten yards apart, wading through water some three feet deep. But as had been the case with many other things they had tried to teach me, it looked a lot easier than it actually was. Having tried and failed at every attempt while the others were spearing fish one after another, I was considering whether to swallow my pride and wade back to shore, when I accidently stepped on a fish that had concealed itself on the sandy bottom. Startled by something big and spiky thrashing and squirming under my foot, in a state of confusion and horrified panic, I drove the spear straight into my toe and let out a howl at the top of my voice. I imagine that if fish could talk and had a sense of humour, my ordeal would be doing the rounds at this very moment and to make matters worse, the men were splitting their sides laughing as I limped back to camp with my tail between my legs. I am glad to say that Connewarre on the other hand was a lot more sympathetic, and dressed my wound with a healing concoction of herbs and leaves.

I made myself scarce for the next two days, and though it took more time than that for my toe to heal, I knew that my wounded pride would take a lot longer to do so. Nevertheless life goes on, and several nights later I had wandered away from the camp to relieve myself, and upon finishing what I came for and turning to go, I was surprised by a young girl standing behind me, staring at me as bold as brass. As I have previously stated ... I am no oil painting, but whatever it was that had led her to follow me, she was making it no secret what she had on her mind. I took a quick guess at her age, reckoning it to be about seventeen years, and as I stood there weighing up what I should do, she took a step in my direction and reached for my hand. As the saying goes ...

it had been a long time between drinks, and with my senses now aroused to such an extent that matters of conscience had no way of competing against lustful desire, I took what I saw as the obvious step, and surrendered myself to the impulse. She took off her cloak … dropping it to her feet without taking her eyes off me for even a second. And as my eyes engaged her in much the same way, the moon shone down, penetrating the branches with fingers of moonbeams as it had done upon countless lovers since the dawn of creation. In spite of her youth, she had a wealth of charms and knew how to use them, and when she lowered her naked body down onto her cloak, I was quick to shed mine and do likewise. Her warm moist mouth … the smoothness of her skin … the soft touch of her hands as she slowly caressed my quivering body … these things and more that I care not to mention all carried me away to unexplored places, and I was a most willing traveller I hasten to add.

By the time the moon had moved on to faraway places, and we awoke to the fear of staying too long, we put on our cloaks before hastily parting, and I sneaked back to camp like a thief in the night. From that night onwards, I thought of her again on many occasions, and as the weeks rolled by one into other, our paths *did* cross again I have to admit. But as fate has done with so many lovers all the way back to Adam and Eve … when the time finally came for the clans to move on, she and her family left along with them, and it near broke my heart as I watched her go.

The sky turned the colour of midnight the day after their departure, and rain pelted us mercilessly for three days and nights. And with no way of keeping a fire alive, we were confined to our lean-tos while they leaked like a sieve. And while the melancholy weather multiplied my gloom one thousand times over, I feared that Noah's flood might be coming to cleanse God's creatures of all of their sins.

I am happy to say however that on *this* occasion, it took just a handful of days for the weather to clear, and when the sun broke through as though all was forgiven, we left to go back to our place by the river.[4]

---

[4] **Footnote.**
The Wathaurong people had occupied the area for thousands of years … referring to it by the Aboriginal name of *Bukor Buloc*. Buckley returned to the place on many occasions over the years, and decades later when white men had come to claim the land, they gave it the name of **Buckley's Falls.**

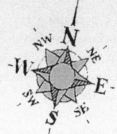

CHAPTER 7
THE NEW YEAR OF 1809

Having now acquired an understanding of their language, I had learnt that a curse had been placed upon the family some years before. Connewarre had told me that when Jillong's wife was a little girl, her father had made an agreement with an older man from another clan that he could have her hand in marriage when she came of age. But the men didn't bargain on the fact that when she grew old enough to think for herself, she would defy their wishes and run away.

Angered by what he took as a personal insult, the man placed a curse upon her and all of her family that had been plaguing their lives ever since. She'd already lost *one* baby as previously mentioned, and as Connewarre continued with the rest of the story, she told me that on the night that Trawalla was born, they very nearly lost *him* as well.

'We were camped by the river when the men were away, and right at the moment when the baby decided to come into this world, the heavens opened up and it rained and it rained like never before. I had placed him in a basket next to his mother and gone out into the storm to bring in enough firewood to last us the night.' She paused for a moment, recalling the event with much trepidation:

'The next thing I knew, the river had turned into a raging monster … knocking me off my feet and very nearly carrying me away in the current. In next to no time, it burst into the lean-to and swept the basket away with the baby in it, before either of us could do a thing about it.' It sounded horrendous to say the least.

'We wailed and we wailed all through the night, and when the storm blew over and the men came back at the break of day, they were carrying the baby and all was well.' She deliberated carefully before adding:

'My husband is a *punjel karne.*'

When I said I had no knowledge of what that meant, her explanation seemed to indicate that he was a type of witch doctor, and with my curiosity now aroused in no uncertain terms, I told her how I had seen him sitting in a tree with a white crow beside him. She replied with: 'My husband's name means *white crow* in your language,' before going on to add: 'He once told me he had a vision that a tall white man would come one day, and that many more would follow to drive us from our land.' The wisdom in her eyes had turned to pools of sadness:

'I hope that you grow to be a very old man Murrungurk.'

I was about to ask her why, when she said:

'Because he said you would be the only one among us who would live to see it.' There were many more questions I would have liked to have asked, but when Jillong's wife came into the lean-to and sat down beside her, I chose not to question her further.

As the days rolled by, I had learnt from a visitor that George Pye had been taken in by one of the clans in much the same manner as had happened to me, and that he had behaved inappropriately with one of their women and had been put to death at the end of a spear. The man had also told me the settlement had been abandoned long ago, and that the ships had sailed and had not returned.

Hearing the news came as no surprise, but it still saddened my heart to hear it.

I was cheered up however the following day, when the others returned from a hunt with a puppy they brought back from a litter they had found. I won't say what they had done with the rest of the litter, other than to point out that the natives considered wild dog a delicacy almost second to none. Nevertheless, Trawalla had convinced his father to spare one pup, and promised to care for it and train it to become a hunting dog. Seeing them playing together over the next few days was a joy to behold, and now that he had other things that required his attention, I decided to go off and spend some time on my own.

Having left the others with a wave of the arm … carrying a spear and enough supplies to last three days, I climbed out of the gorge onto higher ground and paused for a moment to take in the view.

I could see the blue of the ocean glistening off through the morning haze as I gazed around … marvelling at the vastness of a country where one could walk from sunrise to sunset without seeing a soul. And as I stood there trying to take it all in, I noticed the shadow of an eagle hovering above me, cruising majestically over its domain. Having been told by the others that eagles are the *protector spirit* of the Wathaurong people, I turned my gaze skywards watching until it veered off through the glare of the sun before soaring away into the shimmering distance. For no apparent reason, I thought of Connewarre's prophesy of how white men would come and take the land, but with the notion of how greed can turn men into monsters too distasteful a notion to dwell upon, I banished the thought to the back of my mind and set off toward the distant coast.

It was around midmorning by the time I reached the ocean, and I started following the shoreline … covering the same ground that I had travelled back then. And within a couple of hours of easy going, I was crossing the same river that we had crossed at the time. It felt as if time had stood still as I came out of the water to see the same group of huts still standing by the riverbank.

They looked to be a good deal more weather beaten now, and I approached once again for a closer look … wondering if they belonged to some of our clan. Deciding to linger to take some refreshment, I wandered around from hut to hut, recalling as I did so having done the very same thing with Bill and George back when we had been here before on the brink of starvation. Pausing for a moment to reflect upon how much my life had changed since those distant days … as my plan was to visit the island where we had so desperately attempted to attract the ship, and as there were still a few hours of daylight left to travel by, I was back underway in no time at all.

The afternoon was fading fast by the time I had waded out to the island, erected a lean-to and lit up a fire, and as storm clouds rolled in from out at sea … sending me a message that I had better prepare for another wet night, I settled in to await the inevitable. Needless to say, when the rain *did* come, it poured and it poured the whole night long.

As the sun broke through to mark the new day, I awoke to the sound of voices off in the distance, and I looked out from my lean-to over to the mainland and saw a group of natives some twenty-odd strong. Every single one of them was daubed in red paint as though primed for battle … all armed to the teeth and travelling along the beachfront at a cracking pace, as if they were all on a mission and eager to get there. From what I could tell from this far away, they did not appear to be Wathaurong men, but I can guarantee one thing with the utmost certainty … I breathed a sigh of relief when they hurried on by. Wading back onto the mainland when I felt safe to do so, I shuddered at the thought of who their intended target might happen to be and as I took a look around me, I could see that I was standing on the very same beach where Bill and I had said our goodbyes some years before. Pausing to reflect momentarily upon how much my life had changed since then … when I looked down again at the footprints in the sand, I chose to linger no longer and headed off at once in the opposite direction. Now that I'd left the ocean behind, I was making my way up from the coastal plain toward the hills that would lead me back to the campsite. Although I had enjoyed my time alone, I was looking forward to seeing the others again, and in spite of the fact that I made steady progress throughout the day, by the time the sun was sinking low in the sky, I decided to sleep out for one more night. After choosing a site to stop and make camp, I had soon lit a fire and laid my cloak out beside it to serve as a bed. And as the night sounds commenced their familiar chorus,

I sat by the fire watching the sparks climbing skyward into the burgeoning night. Staring into the flames ... my mind drifted back to the days that had passed since having made my escape. Regardless of the fact that it seemed as if nothing had turned out quite the way I had planned, I could now lay claim to feeling as free as a bird.

I lay back marvelling at the galaxy of stars twinkling above, while the old crescent moon ... seemingly unhappy at having lost prime position at the centre of the stage, sulked like a child in a corner of the sky. Glancing across at my dilly bag, I estimated that I had enough supplies to last one more day, and after getting to my feet to throw another piece of firewood onto the flames, I lay back down before being lulled off to sleep by the sounds of the forest.

I awoke to the steely grey sky of the early dawn and wasted no time in getting underway. Aiming to be travelling for most of the morning, I paced myself accordingly ... making steady going that should see me back at our campsite sometime around noon. And as I left the forest and entered a clearing, I came upon a group of kangaroo some twenty yards ahead. Looking up from their grazing having sensed my approach, they watched me with ears twitching for the slightest sounds. I stopped dead in my tracks, thinking of how much praise I would receive if I happened to return to the others with a kill of my own ... and as I made a move to raise my spear, they turned tail and hopped away to the cover of the trees. Disappointed I was although not surprised, and I continued my trek through the rest of the morning, and by the time I rounded a bend in the river a little downstream from where the others were camped, I happened to notice several crows circling above the trees not far up ahead. Feeling a rush of fear come upon me for no apparent reason, I stepped up my pace and the next thing I noticed was the droning of blowflies. A moment later I stumbled upon the body of Connewarre lying dead on the ground in a pool of blood. It felt like I had stepped into the middle of a terrible nightmare, and I went down on my knees with my scream resonating like a banshee's all through the gorge. My head was spinning in a mindless daze as I got to my feet to search for the others... despairing for what I might find. Stumbling onward, I came upon the remains of the one-eyed man with his head and his limbs severed from his body, and as I ran screaming into the clearing, I came upon the bodies of Jillong and his wife tied up together to the trunk of a tree. I had never before felt such despair, and started calling Trawalla's name over and over in the hope that he might have somehow escaped the terrible carnage. As I rushed here and there in a state of panic, I noticed the boy's tumbled-down lean-to and fearing the worst, I looked inside with my heart in my mouth. I broke down and cried ... cursing a God that could be so cruel, while unable to bear the horror I had witnessed, I collapsed to the ground in a pitiful heap. By the time I came to my senses and opened my eyes ... hoping and praying that it had been no more than a terrible dream, what I had awoken to was the grim reality that life as I knew it could never be the same.

It was well after dark by the time I had buried them all, and my hands were bloodied and blistered beyond recognition. I had just endured the worst day of my life, and my tears flowed like a river until I finally gave in to exhaustion and collapsed in a heap at the foot of the graves.[5]

---

[5] **Footnote:**
Buckley made an annual pilgrimage to the site for many years when the yam daisies came into bloom. And after placing a bunch of yam daisy flowers on each of the mounds, he would tend to the graves ... spend the night in the shelter of the old hollow tree, before leaving in the morning when the sun came up.

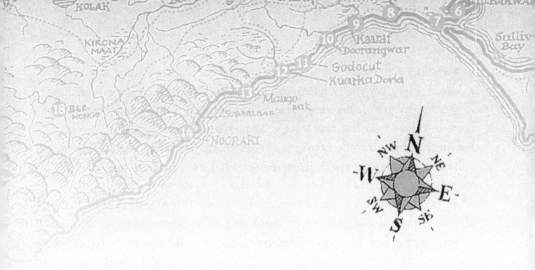

CHAPTER 8

Several months of grieving later

Since the tragic event that had cast me adrift on my own again, I'd taken my hatchet and spear and gone back to the *Kaaraf*... a pretty place by the sea that I'd visited with the others on previous occasions as it had a fresh water spring and an abundance of shellfish growing on the rocks in the tidal shallows. It felt like I was being made to endure a whole lifetime of sadness, and dare I say it ... I even had thoughts of abandoning this world forever. But I managed to maintain my sanity in spite of all that, and as I needed a place to lay my head, I'd built a hut there of more permanent means using logs for a roof that I covered with turf to keep out the weather. There was a tidal creek there too ... running into and out of a salt water lagoon that was fringed around its perimeter by rushes and reeds. As I was walking beside that creek one day, I happened to notice a school of fish swimming upstream with the incoming tide, and though I tried my hand at spearing some, the slippery devils avoided my attempts with relative ease. Standing there dripping water from head to toe ... it occurred to me that if I could somehow manage to dam the creek and block their retreat when they swam back down to return to the sea, it would give me a far better chance of catching one or two when the tide went out. I followed the creek a little further upstream and when I came to a section that was shallow and narrow, I set straight to work at making a dam. Putting my trusty hatchet to good effect, I trimmed some branches from a nearby tree … sharpened the ends as best I could and then hammered them into the sandy bottom. It looked rough and ready I will give you that, but just as long as it could manage to hold firm in the current and prevent the fish from passing through, it mattered not a lick as to how the thing looked.

I had deliberately left a gap in the middle for the fish to swim through, so all that remained was to sit down and wait for the tide to come in. Things seemed to be going the way I had planned, for when the fish swam back and had passed through the opening on their way upstream, I jumped into the water and hammered the rest of the stakes into position. Again I sat around to wait for the tide to turn, and when it finally did so and the water-level dropped … lo and behold … hundreds of fish had been trapped by the dam and were splashing and thrashing about in the shallows. Now that I was able to spear as many as I needed with relative ease, I set straight to work at making a smoke oven. Upon finishing the undertaking by the following day, I now had enough food to serve my needs.

The days drifted by … good days and bad one after another, and I was sitting on the cliff one day staring out to sea, when a dozen or so Wathaurong clan members entered my camp with their hunting dogs trotting beside them. Overjoyed at the opportunity of having human contact again, I greeted them all like long lost friends, and when they asked if they could erect their lean-tos and stay a while … I had no hesitation in saying that they could. There were familiar faces among them although I knew not their names until one of the women introduced herself as Connewarre's sister. When she enquired as to her sibling's whereabouts … alas and alack, she went down on her knees in a flood of tears when I told her the news. Things became chaotic from that moment onwards as the rest of the women began tearing at their hair and crying out in pain, while the men shouted curses and swearing to have their revenge. Swept up once again in a burst of emotion … I felt the grief and the sadness all over again until she reached for my hand and asked if we could sit by the fire and talk some more. As soon as we had sat down, she began reminiscing about the times she and her sister had spent together when they were two little girls:

'Connewarre and I had always been very close. For years, everything we did we would do together,' said she with a tearful smile:

'We were such little devils. We were always getting into mischief.'

She sat for a moment in quiet contemplation before turning to me to say:

'I never knew anyone as stubborn as she was,' as she wiped away a tear with the back of her hand:

'I still recall the day that Darn-Gareeyn-Waa came to our village to ask our father for her hand in marriage. He was so handsome back in those days. He was from another tribe away to the north and was a young man of very high esteem.'

She turned to look me in the eye:

'Our father wanted to say yes to his offer of marriage but Connewarre was headstrong and refused to agree to what they were discussing.'

She turned her gaze toward the flickering flames:

'Back in those days there was a tribe from across the mountains who had often attacked our people without provocation. On more than one occasion our mother had to hide us away in the bushes until the fighting was over and the enemy had gone. When he heard about the attacks, Darn-Gareeyn-Waa promised my father that he could prevent it from happening ever again.'

She paused before adding:

'Not only did Darn-Gareeyn-Waa have a reputation for being the most fearsome warrior in all the land, but both he and our father knew that when a suitor was looking for a girl to marry ... as well as being a good hunter and provider, he should also be able to defend his family in times of trouble.'

She paused again:

'Darn-Gareeyn-Waa was very determined to win his bride, and he promised our father that instead of waiting until the men came to attack our village again, he would take a party of men to seek them out and destroy them first. Then when he had done what he'd promised and removed the threat, he would come back again to marry my sister. I remember the day that Connewarre and I watched them heading off to battle, and when they finally came home all battle-worn and bloodied, Darn-Gareeyn-Waa had lost an eye in the fighting but having done what he'd promised, he so gained a wife.'

Keen to hear more, I decided to say:

'Connewarre once told me that Darn-Gareeyn-Waa had saved Trawalla from drowning on the night the boy was born.'

She grew reflective for a moment:

'My people believe that we share the same spiritual connection as our tribal ancestors, and that their spirits influence every single thing that we do. But in Darn-Gareeyn- Waa's case, he had far more than just a spiritual connection.'

She sat for a while in quiet contemplation:

'Darn-Gareeyn-Waa was different from the rest of us in ways that cannot be explained.'

She turned to look me in the eye:

'For some reason, on the night the baby came into this world, the river spirits came to claim him. But Darn-Gareeyyn-Waa stood up to them and demanded they hand the baby back to its family. The water spirits knew what a great a warrior Darn-Gareeyn-Waa was, and would not agree unless he offered them *his* spirit in exchange for the infant.'

Again she paused:

'Thankfully they came to an agreement and the baby's life was spared.'

I decided to tell her about the night I saw him sitting in the tree with a white crow beside him, and she responded by saying:

'The white crow was his totem. It was said that he could fly to the heavens any time that he wanted.'

She grew reflective again:

'Although there are many of us in the clans that do not like all the fighting and killing, they continue to fight with each other whether we like it or not.'

After pausing to reflect upon how their culture was in certain ways just like my own, I decided to say:

'I too was once a soldier. Our people also go to war against each other and there are often a great many lives lost as a result.'

The distant look returned to her eyes:

'Our people believe that every illness no matter how small ... every accident or every injury does not merely happen by chance.

Our belief is that things are caused by evil spirits or by someone performing acts of sorcery. And when these things happen, a man skilled in the arts of magic will be called upon to identify the culprit so that revenge can be had. That is one of the reasons that our people are always fighting'

Upon noticing that the others were now preparing a meal, she excused herself and got to her feet, saying as she did so:

'I hope we can continue talking later.'

I sat a while longer reflecting upon the things she had talked about. Staring into the flames, I recalled the white crow's vision of how men like me would come to take over the land... oblivious though I was that five hundred miles away in the outlying regions of Sydney town, and two hundred and fifty miles to the south in Van Diemen's Land ... that dream, or perhaps more aptly put ... that *nightmare*, was being played out already with somewhat grizzly effect.

The clan remained with me at the *Karaaf* until the days grew shorter and the nights became cold, and when the time finally came for them to leave the location and move elsewhere, I made up my mind to go along with them.

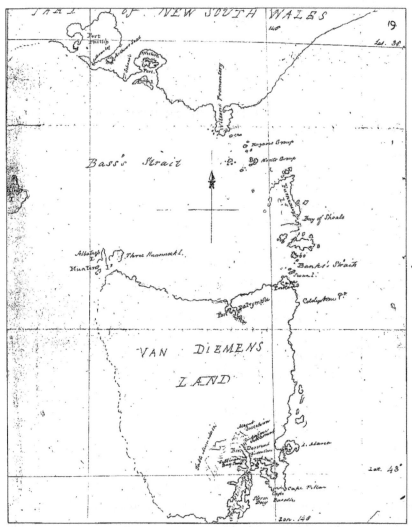

This sketch (indicating the Yarra and Tamar Rivers) which G. P. Harris probably sent to England by the *Ocean* in August 1804, is the first known map of Bass Strait and its surrounding islands to note Sullivan Bay in Port Phillip and Sullivan Bay (Cove) in Hobart Town. It proves that Lieutenant-Governor Collins must have had access to Ensign Barrallier's *Combined Chart of Bass's Straits*, published by Alexander Dalrymple in January 1803, and to Grimes' chart made when he discovered the Yarra. Harris also had at least some knowledge that the French had circumnavigated French Island in Western Port and was with Lieutenant Tuckey during the survey of Port Phillip in October 1803.

Although a very simple effort, the sketch shows a more defined course for the river at Port Dalrymple and also some small islands not shown in the Barrallier and early Flinders charts. This suggests that William Collins and his exploring party also made some contribution to Harris's sketch.

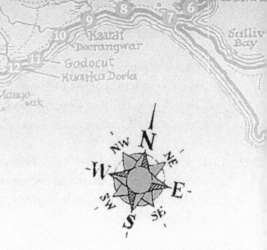

CHAPTER 9

Van Diemen's Land

Science books tell us that the earth has undergone five major Ice Ages over millions of years, with the last one ending some 10,000 years ago. And as the climate warmed and the ocean levels rose, a section of the southeast coast of Australia became isolated from the rest of the continent thereby creating an island 250 miles south of the rest of the landmass. As a result of the separation, the Aboriginal people who had resided in the region for some 40,000 years found themselves cut off from their brethren back on the mainland.

History books tell us that in the seventeenth century the Dutch navigator Abel Tasman had been commissioned by the Dutch East India Company to explore the mysterious southern land they knew by the name of *Terra Australis Incognita,* and upon discovering the aforementioned island in 1642, he gave it the name of Van Diemen's Land. Some one hundred and sixty years later ... due to the fact that there were French ships known to be mapping the region during a time when the British and the French were again at war ... in an attempt to bolster their presence in the region, in the Spring of 1803 the British sent 23 year old Lt John Bowen and a small party of sailors soldiers and settlers to establish a settlement in Van Diemen's Land. Having chosen a site on the banks of the Derwent River, Bowen named the location Risdon Cove. When they'd ensconced themselves, the New South Wales government sent down reinforcements to help bolster the numbers.

Five months later, Governor Collins arrived with his party of 307 Calcutta convicts from the abandoned settlement at Port Phillip Bay, and on the day of their arrival as they sailed upriver, surveyor Harris recorded their approach as follows:

'We are riding snug, about two miles from as beautiful a country in appearance as I have ever seen, and from the great number of fires we see all around, it appears to be tolerably well inhabited."

Harris went on to describe the camp on the following day as follows:

"Our settlement is formed about sixteen miles from the mouth of the Derwent, one of the finest rivers I ever beheld ... deep enough and large enough to admit the entire navy of Great Britain at the one time. The shores rise gradually into hills covered with fine grass and noble trees. We are settled on the left hand side going up in a small cove with an excellent run of fresh water, while the town is built on a fine gently-rising plain." Upon closer inspection however, Governor Collins was not so impressed, and after sending men out to look for a more suitable location, he moved *his* party six miles closer to the harbour mouth to a site that would come to be known as Hobart Town.

Some eight years later when the first census was carried out on Van Diemen's Land, Aboriginal numbers on the island were estimated to have been in the vicinity of 7,000 people, although there were those who considered their numbers to be a great deal more. As was the case on the mainland, these Aborigines had inhabited the region for thousands of years ... hunting and fishing in a way that had enabled them to coexist with nature year after year through good times and bad. With plentiful rainfall, much of the island was lush and green and attracted the animals that grazed on the grasses, and as the Aborigines had long-since learnt how to control the vegetation by selectively burning, they had not only managed to stimulate new growth to attract those animals, but had been able to prevent major bushfires during the harshest of summers. These island Aborigines were made up of nine major tribes ... each with their own distinctive boundaries that had defined their territories since time immemorial. But unlike many other nations that were known to have a history of roaming the earth and sailing the seas in search of plunder, the Aborigines had never sought to conquer anyone. On the contrary ... apart from their customary battles and their tribal disputes, they had been living in relative harmony with the rest of nature for thousands of years.

Like their brothers on the mainland, the island tribes had been free to come and go wherever they pleased within the confines of their tribal boundaries, but as the new arrivals began using hunting dogs and guns to compete for game, not to mention putting up fences and building houses... while it may have seemed to some that the British had found their Garden of Eden, for the original inhabitants it was soon to become a Hell on earth. Just as inevitably as the sun comes up in the morning, tensions began to flare between the blacks and the whites and they exploded with a bang at Risdon Cove.

Several weeks earlier, two twelve pound cannons from Matthew Flinders'

MS Investigator had been taken ashore as a means of defending the British position from a possible threat from the French. Standard naval artillery in battles like the ones that were fought during the Napoleonic Wars, these weapons known as carronades could be used with devastating effect up to a range of four hundred yards. Designed to kill or maim as many of the opposing crew as possible during a naval battle, and therefore similar in effect to a very large shotgun... because of how lethal these weapons were, British seamen had given them the nickname of *"smashers"* and the even more appropriate title of *"the devil's gun."*

The soldiers and convicts at Risdon Cove were proving themselves to be an undisciplined and troublesome lot, and although Collins had been ordered by his superior to take over the command at Risdon, he was busily establishing his *own* settlement six miles downriver at Hobart, and wrote the following message to Governor King in Sydney:

> 'There certainly can no longer be any advantage in maintaining an establishment at Risdon Creek, as I am settled in a much more eligible situation.'

Collins also had a very low opinion of the NSW Corps, and during his earlier years in Sydney he had written in his notes:

"On some evenings, I swear that half the population is in a state of intoxication, and the Rum Corps ... as the New South Wales Corps has come to be known are a disgrace to the flag."

Meanwhile back at Risdon, with threats of mutinous soldiers and a planned convict insurrection, things boiled over while Bowen was away.

Bowen had taken several prisoners back to Sydney after uncovering a plot to rob the settlement stores, and had left Lt William Moore of the New South Wales Corps in charge during his absence. Being a soldier with nine years' service in Sydney during the tensions between the British and the local *Eora* Aboriginal tribes, Moore had long become adept at the practice of shooting first and asking questions later. As stated in Collins' notes, the NSW Corps to which he belonged had gained a reputation for drunkenness and troublesome ways, and like many of his fellows in uniform, Moore had come to regard the natives as a nuisance at best, or at worst ... a serious threat that needed eradicating.

All had been quiet around the camp, while a few hundred yards away tilling the ground for his newly-assigned master ... the convict Edward White had noticed a crowd of natives coming down the valley. Made up of a large party of men, women and children all carrying clubs, they were attempting to drive a mob of kangaroo down the hill in the direction of the stream, and had fanned out in an arc to try to surround their quarry at the water's edge. According to Mister White's statement when he was questioned about it during an enquiry that was belatedly held ... the natives had paid him scant attention and had passed him by as they continued to focus on the job at hand. After having returned to his duties, several minutes later the calm was shattered by an explosion of gunfire as the soldiers opened fire upon the unarmed crowd. Those who were camped six miles away at Hobart Town heard a cannon's boom from somewhere upriver, and all heads turned towards Risdon Cove. Governor Collins wasted no time in sending a messenger to ask for details as to what had occurred, and as Lt William Moore and the surgeon Mountgarrett were the pair who had given the orders to fire their muskets and discharge the cannon, they put *their* version of events down in a letter.

According to them ... four or five hundred natives had been posing a threat to one of the settler's wives, and that they were left with no other choice than to open fire. And although the letter stated that the number of native casualties had been no more than three ... as word quickly spread about the morning's events, there were others who could attest that the dead and the wounded had been a good deal more.

Governor Collins' report to his superior in Sydney included the following excerpt: *'Not having been present myself, I must take it for granted that the measures which were pursued were unavoidable,'* but he was fuming all the same and added the comments:

'I know that they will now consider every white man as their enemy, and will if they have the opportunity revenge the death of their companions upon those who had no share in the attack.'

It would take another 30 years before a committee of enquiry would be held on what had since come to be known as the *Risdon Massacre*. And although no one could know the actual number of Aborigines that had been killed or wounded, the only impartial witness to give evidence to the enquiry was the aforementioned Edward White. With no apparent motive other than to finally have the truth revealed... he stuck to his story that the natives had indeed been posing no threat.

Although that day at Risdon would be the precursor to the violent times to come ... as it occurred during the early days when there were very few Europeans there on the island, it would take another twenty years of intermittent violence before the scales finally tipped against the natives, and they were swept away with incredible force. As for the Risdon Settlement, after Governor Collins received confirmation from Sydney that it was going to be scrapped ... in spite of the fact that he could have used the extra troops at Hobart Town, Collins was fed up with the soldiers troublesome ways and wasted no time in dispatching the lot of them back to Sydney.

As the founder of Hobart, as well as having played a leading role in the colonization of Sydney fifteen years earlier ... Collins played a significant part in early Australian colonial history. Born the son of a high-ranking naval officer in London in 1756, after deciding to follow in his father's footsteps, he'd joined his division as an ensign at the age of fourteen. Collins married the daughter of a wealthy Nova Scotia sea captain at the age of twenty one ... became a captain-lieutenant two years later, before being promoted to captain the following year. Then upon learning that a colony was to be established at Botany Bay, he expressed an interest in being given a role.

When the plans were completed, he was granted the position of deputy judge advocate under Governor Arthur Phillip. Like the other marine officers at the time, he was not allowed to take his wife along so she waved goodbye from the wharf as the ship sailed off with the rest of the fleet, and some eight months after leaving Portsmouth Harbour, the first Fleet arrived at Botany Bay.

Although David Collins and Arthur Phillip shared a compassionate interest in the welfare of the Aboriginals, after a relatively peaceful coming together of the two completely different cultures, violent clashes began to erupt between blacks and whites. Collins had been optimistic in the early days of the settlement ... having noted in his journal:

"It is seldom that men are found existing perfectly in a state of nature which must have once been common to all men."

He'd then gone on to record:

"The Aboriginal people did not seem to regard us as enemies or invaders."

In time however ... with deaths on both sides increasing in number, the pervading atmosphere turned to one of fear and hostility. Collins was one of those who believed that the convicts and sailors were the main protagonists and described them as follows: *"They tend to be callous men of malign intent and little education."* He had little regard for the New South Wales Corps either, and thought them to be even more uncouth and brutish than the convicts.

Some years later he wrote the following words to a friend in England:

"The natives of the Hawkesbury are murdering the settlers, while the soldiers in turn are murdering the natives."

With so much going on around him to assault his senses, he soon turned his attention to the opposite sex. The new object of his affection was Ann Yeats who'd been found guilty of larceny in her native Yorkshire at the age of seventeen, before being transported on the First Fleet for a term of seven years. Ann fell pregnant to one of the ship's seamen before the First Fleet sailed, and gave birth to a son before the ships landed at Botany Bay. Before too long, Ann became Collins' mistress, and bore him a daughter a few months later.

Other than the company of his good friend and mentor Arthur Phillip, Collins' only human contact that gave him any lasting comfort was with Ann and their daughter, and he made no attempt at concealing their relationship or the fact that he'd fathered her child. However, with his day-to-day workload taking up most of his time, he had little opportunity for anything other than sitting on the magistrate's bench, presiding over the criminal court and dealing with all manner of the tasks that being secretary to the governor required of him. Having to constantly deal with those who would choose to break society's rules, he was being bombarded with vice and depravity from every direction, and with the might of the Empire being brought to bear upon the original inhabitants whom he still regarded as innocent savages, he was beginning to view the conflict between blacks and whites with an air of sadness and resignation. With the colony now desperately short of food, sickness on the increase and robberies having reached alarming proportions … his optimism about the future was slowly being eroded with each passing day. To make matters worse, his good friend and mentor Governor Arthur Phillip announced his intention of returning to England. Collins was crestfallen at the thought of losing his closest ally, and when Phillip departed Port Jackson in the December of 1792, Collins would have dearly loved to do likewise, and wrote in his diary that he wished to escape: *"from a country that is no better than a place of banishment for the outcasts of society."*

And while Collins continued to dream of returning to England, Ann Yeats gave birth to his second child. By now she had served out her sentence and was a free woman again, and although she'd grown attached to the colony and wished to remain there and try to forge a new life, Collins made no secret of the fact that he wanted to go home. When he finally got his wish and was able to leave ... he assigned his 100-acre grant of land on the Hawkesbury River over to Ann and the children.

Collins took one last look at the Sydney settlement from the deck of the *Britannia,* before he sailed for England in 1796. What lay ahead was his home and his family, and the wife he had not seen for nine long years.[6]

---

[6] **Footnote.**
With the help of his wife back home in England, Collins used the notes from his diary to write a book entitled: *"An Account of the English Colony in New South Wales,"* before a few short years later, he accepted the offer to head up the settlement planned for Port Phillip Bay.

David Collins, a watercolour miniature by I. T. Barber. The portrait was probably painted shortly before Collins sailed for Port Phillip

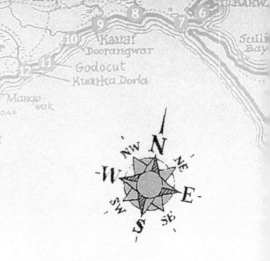

CHAPTER 10

On their exploratory journeys to Bass Strait, Mathew Flinders and George Bass had seen vast seal numbers occupying the many islands throughout the region, and at a time when demand for whale oil was at a premium … there was a school of thought that believed seal oil to be a superior product to that obtained from whales. And as the seal skins were in high demand too, the British administration wasted no time in attempting to capitalise on the enormous potential right there on their doorstep. As word began to spread of the vast fortunes that were seemingly there for the taking, hundreds of sealers were soon working the region. Such was the demand in overseas markets, that in 1804 … one American vessel took 600,000 seal skins in Australian waters, while in another instance … a gang from the brig Harrington based on King Island, slaughtered 4,300 fur seals and 600 sea elephants in one month alone. There were soon any amount of escapees only too willing to turn their hand to the practice for a chance to be free, and the entire region became infested with a raggle taggle assortment of lawless scoundrels who had fled from the settlement … armed themselves with muskets and proceeded to carry out their bloody deeds while being answerable to no one. Governor Collins had originally requested a garrison of

100 marines to support the colony, but had in fact been granted a mere half that number. What's more, because many of the military came from similar backgrounds to the men they were meant to be guarding, they frequently joined in each other's drunken binges when the rum began to flow at the end of the day. Not only did morale become a major cause for concern, but there was a constant struggle to maintain security with so many law-breakers all in one place and no bars or no walls to contain them.

As had been the case back at Port Jackson, a liberal supply of rum in the colony was proving to be a double-edged sword, for in spite of the fact that the practice of doling out spirits was seen as a necessary inducement to help avoid unrest, it led to so much drunken behaviour that it brought a raft of disciplinary problems to go along with it. Van Diemen's Land was being dragged kicking and screaming into the worst aspects of penal life, and the native inhabitants were the poor unfortunates who were bearing the brunt of the forces of change.

Under British law, animals in the wild were deemed to be the property of the Crown, and its laws restricted the right to hunt to a chosen few. But for the Aboriginal people who had been free to hunt whenever they wanted … British laws were no more relevant than their kings or their queens. As a result, what had once largely been a harmonious way of life was being torn asunder right before their eyes. Within four years of the British arrival, the Hobart settlement had become entrenched in the south, and Port Dalrymple … soon to be known by the name of Launceston, was similarly ensconced in the north. And as more and more convicts and settlers were being shipped to the island, the settlements were struggling to support themselves … animal numbers were in a state of decline, and the so-called *'fruits of the earth'* were being stripped from the tree with reckless abandon.

From day one, the convicts had been put to work in accordance with the skills they were deemed to possess, and both Bill Marmon and Dan Mcallenan …

two of William Buckley's fellow escapees from back at Port Phillip, were part of the group who'd been given the job of clearing the forest around the township.

Marmon's views on this were as follows:

I am no longer the man that I used to be since having contracted scurvy back at Port Phillip, so I have been assigned to lighter duties with my young friend Dan.

Because we work in close proximity to those who chop down the trees, and as predicting which way one of these mighty giants is going to fall can so often mean the difference between life and death, we need to be on our guard at all times. Dan has let me in on a secret … he tells me that some of our old Calcutta comrades have been hatching plans for an escape attempt.

I was already aware that the Scotsman David Gibson and his companions had been recaptured following their *last* attempt, and that they had been given three hundred lashes and made to work in irons for one year thereafter. But as that twelve month period is about to expire, they intend to try again.

'The Scotsman's irons come off tomorrow Bill.'

'Yes, I believe that is so,' I replied.

'I was hoping you might change your mind and join us Bill. The boat is in the harbour just there for the taking.'

Dan had been trying to convince me for weeks.

'You know I would under different circumstances Dan, but I have less than a year of my term left to serve.' He gave in without a fight on this occasion … choosing instead to steer the subject on a different course:

'I wonder if William still lives. It must be at least four years since we saw him last.'

Buckley was a man still dear to my heart:

'I have often wondered the same thing Dan. I have thought of him many times since we parted ways.' And as the monotonous thud of the axes ceased their rhythm, and the sounds of the forest began slowly filling the void, someone bellowed a warning that a tree was falling, and with a splitting of timber and a rending of branches that had been blocking its path, the tree crashed down to earth with an earth-shattering thud. As the shower of dust began settling upon the chaotic scene, men came running from every direction as word began to spread that a prisoner had died. 'Stand clear. Stand back and let me pass,' and the redcoat pushed his way through the crowd that was forming.

'Who was it?' somebody asked as he reached down to pick up the hat crushed in the dirt.

'That belonged to young Kelly,' another replied before adding:

'The poor lad was as deaf as post. Probably did not know what hit him.'

The guard began barking orders with little regard:

'Get yourselves back to work. There's nothing can be done for him now … not in this world or the next.'

Dan and I were sitting by the fire when the sun had gone down, while the noise of drunken revelry rang out all around. As I was no longer in the habit of taking strong liquor, I had traded my rum allocation for paper and quill.

'I wish I was able to read and write Bill.'

Dan had been watching me write down my thoughts and proceeded to ask: 'What is it you are writing?'

'Just something I have been thinking about since the boy was killed.'

'Will you read it to me?' Dan was one of the few men here with whom I would share such things, so I looked down at the page and cleared my throat:

'Life is fleeting, fleeting, fleeting and the drums of time are beating, and they're beating, beating, beating as we pass along the road.'

'Did you make that up Bill?'

'Yes.'

He went quiet before saying:

'It's a funny old world Bill.'

'How so?' I asked.

His face had taken on the look of sadness that can weigh a man down and drive him to drink: 'How a young boy can wake up in the morning to a day like any other, and a few hours later … his life has been snuffed out because a tree fell in the forest.'

We sat there in silence as the drunken behaviour displayed its ugly countenance all around the encampment. It barely missed a beat … even as Governor Collins approached the campfire, and he paused for a few quiet words with one of the convicts who was sitting nearby with his wife at his side. Hannah Power's affair with the governor was common knowledge, and when he had said what he'd come for and turned to go … she got up from her husband's side and followed the governor into his hut.

Dan glanced in my direction: 'I have often wondered how Power feels about that.'

'It seems to suit the three of them Dan. And don't forget that it got them a pardon and a fifty acre plot to go along with it.'

'I still think it's a bizarre arrangement nevertheless.'

We had no more to say on the subject, and I returned to my thoughts while Dan returned to his.

Several days later when time and tides were in their favour, five shadowy prisoners made their escape under the cover of darkness.

Dan and I had said our goodbyes, and I had embraced him like a father who was reluctant to let his son go off to war. I lay awake deep into the heart of that moonlit night, turning the same thing over and over again in my head … would I ever get to see my homeland again?

The moon shone down upon the solitary guard sitting by the harbour with his musket in his lap, while the rope which tethered the boat to the tree went taut and then slackened as the waves came and went with little more than a ripple.

A hand reached out and covered his mouth: 'Make a sound and you will be food for the sharks,' as the guard was relieved of his weapon with little ado.

'Hurry now lads,' one man whispered as they hauled the whaleboat closer to shore: 'Ease her out now, and do not touch the oars until we're clear of the beach.' With the musket pointed at the guard as he was hauled on board, someone whispered: 'No need to tell you that any sound will be your last,' and the Scottish voice added: 'Don't be afraid. Your life will be spared if you do what you're told.' The mast was raised with barely a sound and the whale boat glided down the harbour like a swan on a lake. Two of the escapees were seafaring men. One was even rumoured to have saltwater in his veins. They called him the mariner: 'She is a beauty sure and true Dave,' as he ran his hand along her silky-smooth hull: 'Feels like Van Diemen pine. They say it never rots,' while he continued to give her the once-over as though she were a beautiful woman that he longed to possess.

With Dan being the only one aboard who had a fear of the water, he sat alone in the stern battling his demons while the talkative mariner continued his praise: 'Twenty five foot long with a six foot beam if I were asked to hazard a guess.

A sturdy little girl if ever there was one,' as his teeth shone bright in the moonlight like pearly shells on the shore: 'She was made to be rowed, but with this dismountable sail-post she could be racing before the wind in no time at all.'

Although it was he that was doing the talking, it soon became apparent who was in charge when Gibson the Scotsman began to give orders: 'Sou sou-east is our course. And keep her well clear of the breakers. They say the passage is rugged and dangerous,' as he cast a cautious eye in the direction of the surf that was pounding the shore like a rampaging monster. 'We will put into shore just as soon as we are able and not risk our necks out here in the dark.'

With enough rations to last a few days, their intention was to keep travelling south until they reached the end of the landmass that marked the most southerly point of the rugged peninsula. From there, they planned to sail north along the coast until they reached their destination. And with the taste of freedom spurring them on, they put into shore an hour or so later … dragged the boat up onto the sand and secured it with a rope to the trunk of a tree.

'There will be no fires this night for obvious reasons,' the Scotsman advised:

'So I suggest we all curl up together to keep out the chill,' as he tied up the prisoner lest he should try to escape.

'So with half an ounce of luck, we may just find a captain who is willing to take on five extra hands.' He turned his attention back to the chest: 'We have this map and a sextant to show us the way, a trusty spyglass, a flint to light a fire and enough food to last until we have time to catch some of our own.'

After examining the rest of the gear he added: 'We have knives, this six foot harpoon and five strong oars, a trusty sail and a good supply of rope.'

Dan chose that moment to ask a question: 'Is it true that they club the poor things to death when they come out of the water to feed their pups?'

'Hold on for all you are worth. Heave away, haul away, heave away now. It's a watery grave that awaits us if we do not hold our nerve.' Wave upon wave rose up against them … buffeting, pounding without relent, while the men in the boat struggled and strained to pull on the oars for all they were worth. And when it was seeming as if they had given their all and could give no more … as if by some supreme act of divine intervention, the wind dropped to little more than a zephyr, the seas became as smooth as a millpond and a strange eerie calm came to settle upon them. Five exhausted men sat slumped over their oars in disbelief:

'It appears we might just have witnessed a miracle,' the Scotsman muttered as he reached for the spyglass to seek out a beach where they could put into shore. One weary hour later, they were sitting around a campfire counting their blessings while the Scotsman continued to study the map.

Their destination was Schouten's Isle … a tiny speck on the chart, 150 nautical miles to the north, half way up the eastern coast of Van Diemen's land.

No more than eleven square miles in area, it sits a mile offshore from the Freycinet Peninsula … as isolated a place as one could ever imagine.

They sat that night on a lonely stretch of beach with a blazing fire for company, each man reflecting on the day just passed, until the mariner mused:

'Losing an oar was a small price to pay.'

'It could just as easily have been our lives,' added another, while Dan kept to himself … dreading the thought of another day on the water.

They had eaten their fill, the powder was dry and the sky shone bright with a million stars, as the Scotsman came and sat down beside him:

'We came awfully close today Dan, but I feel that the worst is behind us now.'

Dan was able to raise a smile in spite of the way he was feeling:

'I have an awful fear of the water Dave.'

The Scotsman placed an arm around his shoulder: 'You are a brave man Dan. You proved that by joining our group knowing only too well we would be taking on the ocean in an open boat.'

'Thank you Dave. I thought for a while today that I'd be meeting my maker.'

'You and me both Dan … you and me both.'

They'd spent another day and night without event and were back on the water for a third day in a row, when the Scotsman's attention was drawn to the horizon, and he reached for the spyglass for a closer look:

'I think I see our island over yonder.'

They entered a cove an hour or so later and pulled the boat up onto the sand. Standing shoulder to shoulder as they took in the surroundings... they had sailed into a horseshoe-shaped bay of azure blue waters as clear as glass, fringed around its perimeter by a fine narrow margin of golden sand ... as pretty a picture as one is ever likely to behold. 'It looks like a paradise,' one of them marvelled about the idyllic location. 'It may indeed be so, but I feel we should reserve our judgement until we have taken the time to look around,' and just as they were about to do so ... the smell of smoke drifted in with the breeze. 'It appears to be coming from that direction,' the mariner said as he pointed off through the trees while sniffing the air. The Scotsman handed Dan the musket: 'I suggest you stay here and guard the boat Dan,' adding as they readied themselves to go and investigate:

'Stay alert lad. The boat is our lifeline and must be protected whatever the cost.' As they climbed the hill in single file, the smoke was getting thicker with every step, while the stench that accompanied it grew more and more revolting the closer they got. And as they came to the top of the hill and looked down the other side, they saw a smoking caldron sitting over a fire. There were two bark lean-tos off to one side, with a dozen or so barrels stacked up beside them. And while the foulness was bad enough to turn a man's stomach, a dog began barking its disapproval and a bear-like apparition appeared from out of the smoke haze. The Scotsman turned to the others: 'It seems we may have found our sealers camp.'

The mariner turned up his nose: 'It looks more like a rat's lair to me.'

As the Scotsman led them on down the hill, the dog tore into in a frenzy ... foaming at the mouth and throwing itself against its chain as though it would willingly take on the devil himself, and as it continued to do so ... the bear-like creature stared in their direction, observing their approach with scant regard before addressing the Scotsman as they entered his camp:

'Greetings Gibson. The last I heard you'd been clapped in irons.'

Although he was clad entirely in kangaroo skins and with long greasy hair and a scruffy beard that hung down to his chest, the Scotsman recognised him as the escapee John Morey and reluctantly returned the greeting. Morey had been one of the bushranger Richard Lemon's men ... as cold-blooded a killer as ever there was. And as the pair continued sizing each other up and down, the mariner cast his gaze around the camp. Everything he looked at was covered in filth, with a stench so strong you could have cut it with a knife. Scores of seal skins had been staked out to dry, with every last one of them crawling with flies, while out of the corner of his eye he could not help but notice the body of an Aboriginal man strung up by the ankles from the branch of a tree. Straining his eyes for a closer look … he saw a young native girl chained to the tree like a poor frightened rabbit caught in a trap. 'Are you her alone Morey?' the Scotsman enquired.

'No he is not,' a voice replied as a second man stepped out from behind a tree with eyes as cold and as lifeless as a stagnant pond while pointing a musket in their direction. 'This is Baker,' Morey replied: 'We work here together,' before motioning in the direction of the native girl and adding: 'Not that it is *all* work mind you. We have our little play thing here to help pass the time.'

His crude attempt at a smile revealed stained broken teeth through a merciless leer as he cast his beady eyes from one man to another, looking for a sign of amusement which was not forthcoming. The Scotsman knew Morey for the bloodthirsty cur that he was... little more than a wild animal who would sell his own mother if the price were right.

'I assume you have a boat,' Morey enquired.

'Yes we do,' came the Scotsman's reply.

Morey paused … choosing his words as a miser would before spending a pound: 'Perhaps you and your men would care to join us,' sizing the others up and down as he did so: 'If so we could leave the island together and all have a share in the sale of our wares. And there is safety in numbers is there not?'

As wary as a fox that was sensing a trap, the Scotsman replied:

'I will need to discuss it with the rest of the men before I can give you an answer,' and as they turned to go, he added: 'We will talk again soon.'

They talked it over back at the whaleboat: 'There is no telling what he is capable of. He would kill us all if given the chance.' Having stayed behind to guard the boat, Dan was hungry for details: 'And what of the girl that you spoke of?'

'Heaven help the poor young thing,' came one man's reply.

The mariner was in no doubt as to what they should do: 'Heaven be damned.

It would need nothing more than a firm hand to put things right. The poor girl could not have been much more than twelve years old.'

Gibson the Scotsman was deep in thought: 'I would not be surprised if he was watching us at this very moment... counting our numbers and plotting a way to try and turn the situation to his advantage.' He looked in the direction of where the sun was setting: 'I suggest we sleep on it and decide upon a course of action when the new day dawns.'

Quiet returned to the island, but the cold that was descending like an icy blanket could neither erase the stench from their nostrils, nor eradicate the thought of the poor native girl they saw chained to the tree. And as the group settled in for a long cold night ... up on higher ground under the cover of darkness, two desperate men coveted the boat that sat beached on the sand while the campfire flickered through the gathering mist.

The morning peace was broken when Morey burst into their camp gasping for breath: 'Gibson, there's a schooner anchored off shore. They saw our smoke and have come ashore to trade for our wares.' The Scotsman pulled on his boots and the others did likewise: 'So why tell *us*?'

'Because with a few extra hands this could be our chance to be free,' as he outlined his plan just as quickly as he could: 'There are only five of them, and if you and your men were to join with Baker and me ... the seven of us could take over the ship and be sailing for Port Jackson before the new moon.'

His eyes were drawn to the musket: 'And a second weapon would make the task a whole lot easier.' One of Gibson's men chose the moment to ask a question:

'How could we be expected to guard five men all the way to Port Jackson?'

Morey sniggered: 'Who said anything about taking them with us?' before adding: 'Dead men don't talk.' Anxious to be off, he turned to go: 'We need to make haste or the ship will sail without us,' and the others trailed along behind while he rushed on ahead.

The *'Marcia'* was a twenty six ton schooner engaged in the sealing industry around Bass Strait. Long used to trading with sealers under trying conditions ... the crewmen had seen some of the worst aspects of the human condition but on this occasion, even *they* were appalled at what they saw. They had agreed on a price nevertheless, and were loading the skins and the barrels onto the boat when Morey had slipped away to plan their demise.

Dan expressed his doubts to the Scotsman as they brought up the rear:

'Surely you do not intend to be a part of his dastardly plan?'

'Let us wait and see Dan,' and as they came to a halt at the top of the hill, they saw their ticket to freedom lying anchored offshore.

Morey was quick to say: 'Did I not tell you? She is a fine ship, and as good an opportunity as there is ever likely to be. With your men on our side and the element of surprise ... we can surely tip the odds in our favour.'

At that moment Dan felt the need to ask: 'What do you plan to do with the girl?'

Morey was growing impatient: 'The last thing we need is an extra mouth to feed. She is only a savage after all,' and he started hurrying down the hill saying as he did so: 'Come along now, they will sail without us if we delay any longer.'

Dan expressed his concerns as they watched him go:

'He intends to kill them all. Including the girl.'

'Yes that seems to be his plan,' as the Scotsman set off with the others just behind. When Gibson and his men entered the camp, the Marcia crew were gathered at the boat and were about to leave until Morey's accomplice aimed his musket at the captain's head: 'Now don't be in so much of a hurry captain. Why not stay for a while until you get to know us better?'

With only one of the crew members armed with a weapon, Morey disarmed him with ease: 'You weren't planning on using this on *us* I hope,' as he knocked him to the ground with the stock of his musket.

Keen to have the girl released, Dan asked: 'Do you have a key for the lock?'

Morey sneered at the question: 'Now why would that concern you?'

He was becoming cockier by the minute and scowled at the Scotsman:

'Are you with us or not Gibson? Make up your mind and be quick about it.'

You could have cut the air with a knife as all eyes turned in the Scotsman's direction while he stood there giving the sealer an icy stare, and after ever so slowly raising his weapon, he pointed it straight at Morey's chest, saying as he did so: 'I suggest you do what Dan asked and unlock the girl.'

Morey delayed his response … hoping for support from his partner-in-crime that was not forthcoming, and knowing he was outnumbered in every degree, Morey begrudgingly did as he was told and when he had done so, the Scotsman ordered: 'Now cut that man down and dig him a grave.'

You could have heard a pin drop as Morey seemed desperate to stand his ground … his eyes darting left and right like a cornered rat with nowhere to run.

Quickly coming to the conclusion that he did not have a leg to stand on, his face flushed red with an uneasy smile: 'The savage has been dead for over a week.

Why bother with a burial now?' The Scotsman maintained his icy stare:

'Don't make me have to ask you again Morey. Cut him down and bury him.'

When the others had watched on until the job was done, the Scotsman turned to the ship's captain: 'I am afraid we will have to relieve you of your ship,' then added: 'However if you care to go across to the other side of the island, you will find our whale boat with a chart and a sextant, as well as enough supplies to get you and your men to Port Dalrymple.'

He then gave Dan an encouraging smile: 'How would you like to give our two sealers some of their own medicine?'

After they'd chained the pair up to the tree and thrown the key away into the surf, Gibson and his men climbed into the longboat and rowed out to where the schooner awaited.[7]

---

[7] **Footnotes:**

The Scotsman and his men were apprehended several weeks later and charged with piracy before a Vice Admiralty Court in Port Jackson and were sentenced to hang. However, following a petition from the ship's captain for the way in which he and his crew had been mercifully treated, the men's lives were spared and they were permitted to serve out their time back in Hobart Town. Morey and Baker were not so fortunate, and swung from the gallows for the crimes they'd committed.

Although nothing is known of what became of the mariner, Bill Marmon finally got his wish and was able to return home to England when he'd served out his sentence the following year.

Dan McAllenan *also* served out his time, and having done so … he got to go back to his native Ireland.

David Gibson the Scotsman was pardoned in 1813, and was to remain in Van Diemen's Land for the rest of his life. He went on to become one of the largest landowners in the north of the island … became a highly successful pastoralist and a prize-winning breeder of merino sheep. He married Elizabeth Hayward in 1819 … the daughter of First Fleet convict parents, and the home they built on the banks of the South Esk River at Evandale still bears the original name of *'Pleasant Banks'* to this very day. He and Elizabeth raised ten children, and he died aged 82 in 1858.

Hobart Town, c. 1806. The governor's house (No. 1) is in the centre foreground next to the Printing Office (No. 6)

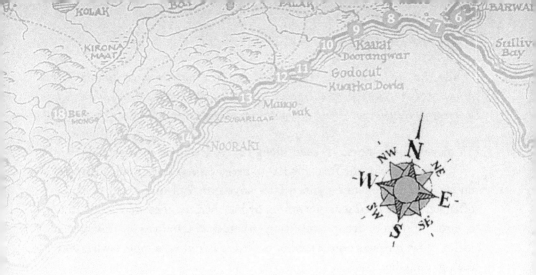

CHAPTER 11

Six years after arriving in Van Diemen's Land, Lt Governor Collins ended his affair with his mistress Hannah Power and formed a liaison with Margaret Eddington … the daughter of a convict-settler from Norfolk Island, and she bore him a daughter later that year. Collins' health however was about to fail him, and after contracting an illness just three months later, he failed to recover and died unexpectedly at the age of fifty four.

Even under a new Governor, store ships from Sydney had failed to arrive, and as the hunting grounds nearby had been largely exhausted, a number of convicts had been armed with weapons and dogs and sent out into the countryside to look further afield in search of game. And by the time store ships *did* start arriving, most of the hunters had become so adept at bush survival that they were reluctant to give up their new-found freedom and had started attacking the natives and stealing their women, as well as assaulting and robbing the defenceless settlers.

During this troublesome period, the commandant at Port Dalrymple had been recorded as saying: *"Bushrangers have been committing unspeakable cruelties against both the natives and others."*

While the surveyor G.P. Harris agreed: *"The natives were quiet if left unmolested, but escaped prisoners have wantonly murdered them and taken their women, whereupon the Aborigines naturally sought revenge."*

To make matters worse ... even though there were not enough soldiers to protect the citizens, the first convicts to be sent *direct* from England arrived on the island, soon to be joined by a large group of undisciplined repeat offenders who'd been sent down from Sydney because they were too hard to control. With both groups consisting of hardened criminals ... this sudden influx of lawbreakers only served to make the island even more lawless with each passing day.

There'd been a succession of governors after Collins' death, and when Colonel George Arthur was appointed to the role, he took on the task of defeating the outlaws as a number one priority. Engaging black trackers from Port Jackson to act as guides to track them down, and by offering rewards pardons and land grants to anyone who could bring in a bandit dead or alive... the tide began turning against them until slowly but surely, one after another the last of the bandits were brought to heel.

Order might have been restored at that point, but no sooner had *one* dilemma been overcome, when the issue of Aboriginal violence took over as the major concern. There'd been sporadic flare-ups between blacks and whites for the past twenty years, but with the best Aboriginal hunting grounds now off limits having been given away as land grants ... as those settlers began putting up fences, building their houses and planting their crops, friction between blacks and whites became worse and worse. It had taken some time for the Aborigines to grasp the magnitude of the changes that were being inflicted upon them, but when they finally did so, they began to fight back with deadly force.

The **Black War** as it came to be known, raged unchecked across most of Southern Van Diemen's Land from the east coast to the midlands for the next eight years, and with no man woman or child able to sleep soundly in their beds ... Arthur had to act and act he did. With the knowledge fresh in his mind of how they'd beaten the bushrangers, a plan was devised to form *roving parties* to go out and hunt down the natives by whatever means they could, and they were soon scouring the countryside wreaking havoc all over the island. Made up of a dozen or so soldiers, settlers and convicts ... they were given free rein to roam far and wide and seek them out. Their main tactic was to locate the smoke from native campfires or the glow of their fires when the sun went down, then they'd ambush the unsuspecting Aborigines with often lethal results. With the natives responding by killing the settlers ... burning their huts and destroying their stock, the fight raged on unchecked with casualties on both sides continuing to climb.

In the early days of the conflict, the *Colonial Times* had been critical of the government policy which it saw as: *"Empowering a class of people so notoriously ignorant and uneducated as most of the settlers are, to hunt down and destroy their fellow man."*

But as Aboriginal attacks continued and the death toll climbed, the paper changed its tune and had instead begun to argue: *"We say unequivocally, self-defence is the first law of nature, and the government must remove the natives. If not they will be hunted down like wild beasts and destroyed."*

Along similar lines, the *Hobart Town Courier* wrote: *"The Aborigines have formed a systematic plan for carrying on a war of extermination against the white inhabitants of the colony."*

While this was going on, Governor Arthur had appointed a man named George Augustus Robinson to act as overseer for an experimental Aboriginal depot on Bruny Island near the mouth of the Derwent. Concerned about the rising violence, Arthur had begun a plan of conciliation to supply a small group of Aboriginals with blankets and rations under the supervision of a soldier and three trusted convicts. He also devised a scheme for the government to pay a five pound bounty per native to anyone who could bring them in unharmed. As a response, Robinson put together a party of trusted natives and fourteen bush-wise convicts and embarked upon a so-called friendly mission to travel around the island contacting the tribes. His original plan had been to offer gifts and food in the hope of enticing them back to Bruny Island where they could be taught to be good Christians and to live like Europeans. To achieve his ends, Robinson made them a promise that if they came into captivity, they would be given a safe place to live and be fed and clothed and be able to return to their homeland when things settled down. And while he and his party were travelling the countryside giving assurances that he was in no position to *give* let alone keep, much of the interior was crawling with roving parties and vigilantes, armed to the teeth and baying for blood.

While all this was going ... in the far north-west corner of the island, a chartered enterprise known as the Van Diemen's Land Company had been granted 250,000 acres of land for the grazing of sheep.

The area had been named Cape Grim thirty years earlier by Mathew Flinders when he sailed by in the *Norfolk* on his journeys of exploration. With a native population of some six to seven hundred men women and children, up to that point they'd lived there in relative isolation from other island tribes. When the Van Diemen's Land Company survey team had first arrived, they'd found the natives to have been entirely peaceful. But like what had occurred up to now in other parts of the island ... with so many men and no available women, trouble flared up in no time at all. Within weeks of their arrival, one of the company's workers reported that some of the shepherds: *"Had designs of violating the native women,"* and it was then reported that: *"a female Aborigine had been kept by a stock-keeper for a month. After which time she was taken out and shot."*

With similar incidents occurring one after another, the tribe sought revenge by destroying a flock of the company's ewes and throwing their carcasses over a cliff.

What the company men did in response would become known as the *Cape Grim Massacre,* and it would take a further two years for Governor Arthur to hear an account of what had occurred. When it all came out, one of the perpetrators told the Governor's emissary: *"We threw the Aborigines' bodies down onto the rocks where they'd thrown the sheep."* A second version of events came from another one of those who'd been involved in the killings, and who bragged that he and three other men had come upon a party of blacks collecting shellfish at the bottom of a cliff, and had opened fire upon them from up above and killed as many as thirty. An *independent* report of what had occurred came from Rosalie Hare ... the wife of a ship's captain of a vessel which had sailed out from England to visit the Van Diemen's Land Company holdings. During her eight week stay, she wrote in her journal: *"Natives are terrible robbers and do all the mischief they can to the settlers ... burning the huts of the shepherds and stealing their dogs are also the works of these incendiaries, but we are not to suppose the Europeans in their turn take no revenge. We have to lament that our own countrymen consider the massacre of these people an honour. While we remained at*

Circular Head there were several accounts of considerable numbers of natives having been shot by the company men, they wishing to extirpate them entirely."

Her letter went on to say: *"The master of the company's cutter assisted by four shepherds and his crew, surprised a party and killed twelve of their number."*

And while native numbers were in decline all over the island, settlers continued coming by the shipload in search of their El Dorado.

John Batman for example had come down from Parramatta several years earlier with his brother Henry and several Sydney blacks he had in his employ. Allocated six hundred acres of land in the Fingal district near mount Ben Lomond, he was one of those who turned his hand to tracking the bushrangers. Then when the native conflict began to flare up, he formed his own roving party with the aid of his Sydney black trackers. If you were to disregard what was happening to the unfortunate natives … things seemed to be going to plan, and it didn't take long for Governor Arthur to inform the Colonial Office that he had: *"received encouraging reports from the two parties I have employed on an embassy of conciliation … Robinson in the southeast, and Batman in the northeast."*

Robinson however seemed to be the only one on the island who was attempting the task by non-violent means, and after one or two years more of continuing slaughter, there were very few natives left at all. For those that *were* … the Aboriginal Committee made the decision to send the last of their number to Flinders Island, having stated in their report:

"From Flinders Island escape is quite impossible."

In summary … it had taken a mere thirty years to drive one of the world's most ancient civilisations to the brink of destruction, for their numbers by then were virtually zero, and that as they say was that.[8]

---

[8] **Footnote.**
The following definitions are from the Oxford English Dictionary:
"Invasion:"
"The action of invading a country or territory, especially with armed force:"
"Massacre:"
"To cruelly or violently kill; to make a general slaughter."

CHAPTER 12

Depending upon who you were to ask at the time, government policy towards the Van Diemen's Land's natives had either been a complete fiasco or a huge success. Whatever the case, it seemed as though things had been settled once and for all. For John Batman however things were far from settled. He had heard the glowing reports to have come out of Hume and Hovell's journey of exploration from Sydney down to Port Phillip Bay, where they'd passed through what they described as millions of acres of magnificent pastoral land with plenty of fresh water to go along with it. This was at a time when all the best agricultural land in Van Diemen's Land had become both scarce and costly.

Said to have been a restless romantic with big ambitions, Batman began to dream of how much better life could be in this new and exciting land. Now in his thirties, a family man with a wife who would bear him six daughters in quick succession, he was also suffering from cerebral syphilis … the disease that would take his life just a few years later.

Batman had been described by one historian as being:

"A tough extroverted charmer, who was kind generous and honest, but was also liable to drink too much and to whore indiscriminately."

In whatever way you might wish to describe him, he had met the colony's assistant surveyor John Wedge a few years earlier when Wedge was marking boundaries near Batman's land, and the pair struck up an immediate friendship.

It didn't take long before they'd started working on a plan to form a syndicate and cross the straits to purchase some of that land from the natives there.

Having heard that the Henty family was *also* planning to settle on the mainland ... with his health by now in a state of decline, Batman knew in his heart he had no time to lose. Not only did he have the *dream*, but with the Sydney natives that he had in his employ and his knowledge and experience of Aboriginal people, he felt in his heart that he was up to the task.

Although he had come from convict stock, Batman had earned a degree of acceptance with the government for services rendered in the campaigns against the bushrangers and his dealings with the natives. And with Wedge as an ally, they began to explore ways of obtaining the money and the political support they would need if they were going to turn their dream into reality. They would be needing a powerful syndicate of that they were certain, and the men they went after were carefully targeted. The first was Joseph Gellibrand. Not only was he one of Van Diemen's Land's leading lawyers, but he was the former Attorney-General of the island. Gellibrand not only had the legal expertise to draft their agreement, but he was also acutely aware of Aboriginal issues. Another key person to join their syndicate was Charles Swanston. As a member of the Legislative Council, he was an ally of Governor Arthur, and in addition to that ... he was a leading banker who could help raise the funds. Each person had to have specific skills and contacts to help their cause, and as their membership grew, the fifteen members of the Port Phillip Association as it came to be known were gradually gaining the political and economic influence to achieve their ends. With what had happened in the case of the Van Diemen's Land natives as a perfect example of what *not* to do ... one of their foundation rules was that an agreement with the Aborigines would have to be an essential component, and that any agreement would need to be based upon a treaty that would take the natives' welfare into account.

Although the syndicate was making steady progress, they were not moving *fast* enough for Batman, and in spite of the fact that not all of the shareholders were as yet formally signed up, Batman was fearful that time was slipping away, so he chose to act at once and crossed the strait regardless.

On Friday 15th of May, the *Tasmanian* newspaper recorded:

"Mr Batman proceeded on Sunday last, in the sloop "Rebecca" from Launceston to Port Phillip, with the first part of his expedition to form an establishment on that part of the continent of New Holland. He takes with him seven natives and three English servants.

He proposes to purchase from the chiefs of that part of the country such a territory as he may require, of which he will himself become the chief, with the best of all possible titles, that of real proprietor. He returns for his family – Mrs Batman and their daughters as soon as he is established."

Following a rough crossing that had taken them longer than expected, they came through the *"Heads"* on Friday May 29th 1835 and anchored in a small sheltered bay before going ashore to explore.

The following extracts have been taken from his journal:

<u>Saturday May 30th 1835:</u>

'I found the countryside of a most superior description – beyond my most sanguine expectations. The land excellent, and very rich – and light black soil, covered with kangaroo grass two feet high, and as thick as it could stand. Good hay could be made and in any quantity. The trees not more than six to the acre, and those small she oak and wattle. I never saw anything equal to the land in my life.'

<u>Sunday, May 31st:</u>

'Saw a tribe and got up to them about one o'clock P.M. They seemed quite pleased with my natives, who could partially understand them. They came back with us where I gave them eight pairs of blankets, thirty handkerchiefs, one tomahawk, eighteen necklaces and beads, six pounds of sugar, twelve looking-glasses, and a quantity of apples, which they seemed well pleased with.'

Monday, June 1st:

'We left the vessel this morning at daybreak. The only thing that will be felt on these plains will be the want of timber. There is none that is fit for sawing or splitting. These extensive plains I have named Arthur's Plains.

This day it rained nearly the whole of the time we were out, with a hailstorm, and the wind blowing hard from the west – very cold.'

Tuesday, June 2nd:

'This morning the natives came on board to pack up for a start, but owing to the rain and the fog, we could not see any distance before us, and it would be very uncomfortable travelling.'

Wednesday, June 3rd:

'After getting everything ready this morning, left the vessel about 9 o'clock, and went up the river. On both sides the land is open and covered with excellent kangaroo grass. The river varies from one hundred yards to sixty yards up it. I have named this place Gumm's Well.'

Thursday, June 4th:

'Started this morning up the river. Most beautiful sheep pasturage I ever saw in my life. Followed on and when we made the river again, stopped for the night in a corner alongside that river.'

Friday, June 5th:

'Left the river this morning for west-north-west direction. I intend to cross some large plains. The whole land I have passed up to this time is, as usual, very good, and plains seem twenty and thirty miles distant. We have just seen the smoke of the natives in an easterly direction, and going to take that course. This land I think was richer than any high land I have seen before. We came on to a small valley, and, to our joy, found a tea tree scrub at the upper end of a small creek running south-east. Here we found good water at sunset, and remained for the night.'

<u>Saturday, June 6th:</u>

'Started this morning at 8 am to find the natives. We walked about eight miles and shortly came up with a family – one chief, his wife, and three children. I gave him a pair of blankets, handkerchiefs, beads and three knives. He then went on with us, saying he would take us to the tribe, and mentioned the names of chiefs. We walked about eight miles where we were joined by eight men armed with spears, who took us with them to their village. After some time and full explanation, I found eight chiefs amongst them, who possessed the whole of the country near Port Phillip. After a full explanation of what my object was, I purchased two large tracts of land from them – about six hundred thousand acres more or less.

I delivered over to them blankets, knives, looking-glasses, tomahawks, beads, scissors, flour etc, as payment for the land. Also agreed to give them a tribute, or rent, annually. The parchment the eight chiefs signed this afternoon, delivering to me some of the soil of each of them, as giving me full possession of the tracts of land.'

There were two treaties, each executed on parchment in triplicate. The first covered some 500,000 acres. This was known as the Melbourne treaty, while the second treaty ceded 100,000 acres of the Geelong, Indented Heads area. During this time, the region was inhabited by three Aboriginal groups. One being the Wurundjeri, who occupied the land surrounding the Yarra River and all of its tributaries. The second were the Bunurong, who lived on the Mornington Peninsula and around Westernport Bay. The Wathaurong were Buckley's people, they occupied the land to the west on the Bellarine Peninsula and up into the Otway Ranges. Along with two other tribes, they comprised what is known as the Kulin nation. Said to have been made up of some fifty to one hundred thousand men women and children, they were governed by senior elders who were the custodians of the law and had the authority to represent their groups in all matters of importance.

Now that Batman had achieved what he set out to accomplish, he returned to his newly-acquired land at Indented Head, where he left some of his party with three hunting dogs … three months' supply of meat, flour and sugar as well as three hundred and fifty eight pound of potatoes, before he set sail for Launceston to carry the news. The men he left behind consisted of James Gumm and Alexander Thompson who were Batman's servants, along with William Todd, a legal clerk who'd joined the expedition to help complete the deed, and last but not least ... his Sydney natives. Batman had left explicit instructions for his men to develop friendly relations with any local natives that they might come into contact with, and the men set to work at preparing a farm until he returned. Tents were erected and a vegetable garden and orchard was prepared, and when the garden site was cleared and the boundary fenced ... vegetables were planted.

After the visitors had been toiling there for about two weeks, a group of five Aboriginal men entered their camp and were given gifts of scissors, knives and blankets. Quickly having decided that they were on a good thing ... two of their number left to bring back the rest of the tribe, and a day or two later, another sixty or so had arrived to join them. In an effort to maintain friendly relations, they were given nearly *all* of the presents there were left to give, and William Todd recorded in his journal on the following day:

"Baked 100lbs of flour for them in small dampers which they soon demolished, being very hungry. In the evening sixteen of the men Corrobbering. They then had their supper and retired to their huts for the night. They consumed most of our potatoes. We kept watch all night."

Three days later he wrote:

"Natives still with us – find it very difficult to get them to leave us. They having taken such a particular liking to the bread, we are obliged to use none ourselves on acct of their distressing us – They being of such a greedy disposition that they would take it all from us. Stopped all night watching as usual."

He then wrote again on the following day:

"Tried all we could to get them to leave us, but found it impossible. Three hands obliged to go Cangarooing. All hands without breakfast so as to shew them we have got no more to give them. Returned home with two Cangaroo; remained all night quiet and well satisfied, but seem to have no idea of leaving us, which makes us exceedingly uncomfortable, not being able to get a meal of Victuals in comfort & always obliged for our own safety to keep watch."

After five more days, Todd recorded in his diary on Sunday 6th of July 1835:

"About 2 o'clock, a white man came walking up to the native huts, a most surprising height. Clad the same as the natives. He seemed very pleased to see us. We brought him a piece of bread which he ate very heartily. Jim measured his height, which was six foot eight inches. He told us his name was William Buckley."

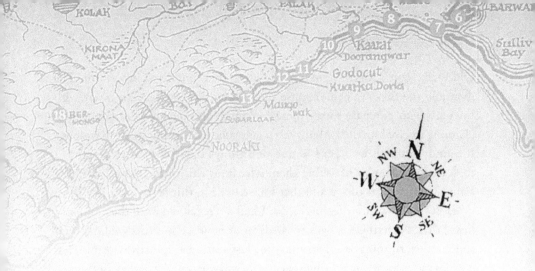

CHAPTER 13

Once again I find myself standing on the outside looking in ... having just returned to what some might refer to as civilisation. I am feeling torn between what has been my way of life for many years now, and a world which has become like a stranger to me.

What has led to this situation? ... Yesterday I came upon a pair of Wathaurong tribesmen who told me they'd discovered a party of white men camped near the coast. And after showing me an axe they had stolen from them, they said they were going to fetch the rest of their tribe so they could go back and kill the whites then help themselves to the rest of their supplies. I know the Wathaurong people well enough to take such a threat with the utmost seriousness, for I have witnessed enough of their warring and fighting to last me a lifetime.

So I have come to the whites' camp to try to prevent any bloodshed.

My other concern is that as an escaped felon, I fear that coming back to a white man's world could have the effect of leading me to the gallows, so I have told them I am a survivor from a shipwreck that foundered in a storm. The men told me they are here because their leader has negotiated a treaty with the natives to purchase some Aboriginal land, and one of them has a letter claiming to give him the authority to put anyone off that might try to trespass. It sounds odd, but who am I to question things that I do not understand? I took the opportunity of asking them what year this is, so I now know that I am fifty five years of age and that I have lived in this place for thirty three years. It's a very strange feeling ... for I had never felt old until the moment I heard that. Nevertheless, back to the issue at hand. The settlers tell me their supplies are running low and may not last until a ship arrives. And what worries me most about hearing that ... is that knowing the natives in the way that I do, they will not be impressed when the gifts start running out, so I have warned Mister Todd and the others to be on their guard.

Mister Todd wrote in his journal later that night:

"Being a long time with the Natives, Buckley has nearly forgot the English language – but the Native language he can speak fluently. We brought him to our tent. Clothed him with the best we had, & made him share the same as we."

Batman's party was made up of James Gumm, William Todd, Alexander Thompson and seven Sydney natives that were in Batman's employ. He had left them with three months' supply of food and provisions and an assortment of fruit and vegetable seeds to plant. Their instructions were to prepare a farm and a cottage and fence it all off whilst paying particular attention to the wellbeing of the natives. Meanwhile back in Van Diemen's Land, Batman had put a cat among the pigeons with the British powers-that-be, and there was much to-ing and fro-ing between those in authority as they tried to determine the validity of the treaty. While all this activity was going on, Batman's health had become considerably worse, so he'd asked John Wedge to go to Port Phillip and begin the process of surveying their land.

Back at Port Phillip, Todd recorded in his diary:

"Buckley has informed us that when those two men which had met him at the heads, after they told him we were here, they stated that it was the intention of the remainder of the Mob that they left behind was going to rush our tent at night

for the purpose of killing us for our provisions. He told them that if they attempted anything of the kind, we should destroy every one of them."

News was spreading fast about the rich pasture land that was seemingly there for the taking, and there was no shortage of settlers willing and eager to cross the strait in the hope of claiming some for themselves. John Wedge was the first to arrive with Henry Batman, his wife and their four little daughters. Then several days later, John Pascoe Fawkner's *Enterprise* was the next vessel to enter the bay. And when the sloop *Endeavour* arrived in quick succession, the race seemed to be on in earnest. Meanwhile Buckley had revealed the truth about his convict background, and Wedge had promised to try and get him a pardon.

Wedge wrote to a fellow member of the Port Phillip Association shortly after arriving at Batman's camp:

"The men left here had been out of provisions for 10 days, having subsisted principally upon roots, with now and then a kangaroo. I found about 46 natives, men women and children at the establishment and a white man of the name of William Buckley who had been living with the natives ever since the abandonment of the original settlement. Buckley says that the tribe are few in number, that they do not much exceed 100 – They are divided and wander about in families and there is no such thing as chieftainship amongst them – but this is a secret that must I suppose be kept to ourselves or it may affect the deed of conveyance if there should be any validity in it. With respect to Buckley, if you and the other gentlemen should consider the obtaining his free pardon to be of the same importance as to ensuring the success of our enterprise as I do, you will see the importance of using every exertion individually and collectively to obtain it for him, and I beg most earnestly to recommend his petition to the favourable consideration of His Excellency the Lieutenant Governor. In doing so I scarcely need advert to the danger that would ensue to the lives of those who may in future reside here by his being driven to despair by the refusal of his petition which would probably induce him to join the natives again; and in which event there is no calculating on the mischief that might ensue by the hostile feelings that he would have it in his power to instil in the breasts of the natives."

Mister Wedge has engaged me as a guide on his second expedition with four of the Sydney blacks Mister Batman has in his employ, and having got to the end of this first day of trekking, we were sitting around the campfire when Mister Wedge made the comment:

'Your story is a remarkable one William.'

I saw nothing special in what I had done, so I responded accordingly:

'All I did was stay alive. I see nothing remarkable in that.'

Being keen to gain some knowledge of what had occurred since I'd made my escape, I asked what had happened after the Sullivan Cove settlement had been moved to Van Diemen's Land.

The stories he told me saddened me deeply, and I had been deep in thought when I turned to him and said: 'I find it hard to imagine how an entire race can be wiped off the face off the earth in little more than thirty years.'

He threw another branch onto the fire:

'Yes it is a horrible tragedy I have to agree. And it will not be repeated here I can assure you of that. That is why we have chosen to negotiate a treaty ... so the settlers and the natives can all agree upon amicable terms of settlement.'

'Do you really believe that the natives understand what it is they are agreeing to?' It seemed that he did based upon his reply: 'The world is getting smaller William. As an Englishman, you know as well as I do that people have been sailing the seas for hundreds of years, trading their wares with other nations. And in the process of doing so, visitors from other lands sometimes settle in those places and carve out a harmonious future there. Better the British than the French I hasten to say.'

'But there is a big difference between the picture you are painting, and the senseless slaughter of innocent people.'

'No one would disagree with you about that William. That is why our association has chosen the road of negotiation as opposed to one of force. In Van Diemen's Land, the settlers found the land empty and untilled. Not *every* one of them spoke through the barrel of a gun, and not every one of them were thieves either.

I could see that he was determined to make his point as he went on to add:

'I have heard it said that the native people do not *own* the land as such. They merely travel over it.'

'Yes they *do* travel over it, but it is so much more than that. The land is vital to them. In fact it *is* them. It is *who* they are. It is the spirit of their ancestors. Without the land they are nothing at all.'

I paused to give the subject a little more thought, before going on to say:

'As a convict, I know what it's like to steal. You simply take something that doesn't belong to you. You don't have to know who *owns* it for it be considered a crime.'

He looked up from the fire and his gaze met mine:

'That is true William, but there are also many of us who believe in paying a fair price for that which we take.'

He fell silent for a moment as he stared into the flames:

'Regardless of what you might think of me and those that I represent, you can rest assured that I will do everything in my power to try to get you your pardon. Now let's try to get some sleep. We have a full day's travel ahead of us tomorrow.'

This part of this country they claimed to have purchased, included all of the land for forty miles west of the place that the natives call *Beangala*, but Mister Wedge and his men have named Indented Head … and every square inch is Wathaurong land. Having lived as I did for my first twenty-odd years in a white man's world, I had seen and used their weapons of war, and experienced their greed and their ignorance. And now that I was back to wearing white men's clothes, I lay awake thinking which side of the fence I would find myself on, before I finally fell into a restless sleep with Connewarre's prophesy repeating over and over, every fretful minute of my haunted night: *"White men will come and take our land … white men will come and take our land,"* while a ghostly apparition of my native family drifted along endlessly through my tormented dreams:

"White men will come and take our land."

Another day has dawned and Mister Wedge is again keen to be on our way:

'You must know this territory like the back of your hand William. The river that you mentioned last night … is it far away?'

'Not far. Perhaps two hours or so in a south-westerly direction.'

'And the lakes?'

'About the same.'

'Then let us make haste. I am looking forward to discovering all there is to see.'

Although I was finding little comfort in travelling as we were through a cold and wet morning, Mister Wedge on the other hand was so fascinated by everything around him, that all he could see was sunshine and roses:

'It is wonderful William. It's the most beautiful countryside I ever did see,' and he had paused once again to sketch in his field book. Just as did so, the shadow of an enormous bird began soaring majestically directly above us.

'Look William. I think it's an eagle.'

'Yes, the Wathaurong call them *bugal bunjil*. Eagles are their spirit being … their creator spirit. They are very sacred to them.'

'Amazing William. Quite amazing,' as he made another note in his journal then put it away in his rucksack and got to his feet to move on.

The weather was becoming more and more miserable the further we went, but in spite of it all, he seemed to be enjoying himself all the more.

'How much further to the lake William?'

'Perhaps another hour or so.'

'What did you say they call it?'

'Connewarre. It means swans on the water.'

I was just about to tell him that it was also the name of the lady who'd saved me, but the moment was lost when he quickly ducked behind a tree to relieve himself.

We had passed through a forest a short time later, and could now see the river just up ahead, and right at the moment we'd started heading upstream, the rain began falling in earnest.

We had taken shelter under a tree and were looking out upon the river when he turned to me and asked: 'What do they call it William?'

'*Barre warre,* or *barwurn*. It means *from the hills to the sea.*'

'How long is it do you think?'

'I'm not really sure. Perhaps a hundred miles or so,' adding as I stood watching the rain coming down in torrents: 'It can get a little salty down in the lower reaches because it's tidal, but you can generally find fresh water if you know where to look.' To pass the time, I pointed to the tree we were standing beside: 'See this scar in the tree trunk? That's where a tribesman would have cut out a piece of its bark so he could build himself a canoe. I have seen them do it on many occasions. They fold the ends over and tie them up with kangaroo sinew.'

Once again he began scribbling notes in his journal, saying as he did so:

'Ingenious William. Quite ingenious.'

'Yes, the Wathaurong are known as water people.'

'I see. Quite amazing William. Quite amazing indeed.'

He'd turned his attention back to taking our bearings, and when he had finished I decided to ask: 'What sort of compass is it?'

'A surveyor's compass. It's a fine piece of equipment if ever there was one.'

He confirmed the fact that he took pride in his work by going on to say:

'It enables the horizontal and vertical angles of an objective to be measured simultaneously with reference to an assumed horizontal plane and an assumed azimuth direction.' Though I nodded my head as if I understood every word … I was sorry I'd asked, and because the rain had just stopped just as quickly as it had started, this time it was *I* who suggested moving on.

We'd followed the river's twists and turns for several miles when we came to the lake I'd been talking about. And as we stood there on the bank taking in the surroundings … it looked as if every single waterbird for miles around had dropped by for a visit, and each and every one of them had something to say.

This was a place that was dear to my heart: 'This whole area around here is Bengali land. They're a Wathaurong clan.' I pointed to a part of the lake where the waterway narrowed just near the place where the river flowed in:

'See where it narrows there into a channel and the trees close in on either side?' He nodded his head. 'I have stood here and watched them catch birds by the dozen. They string a net from one side of the river across to the other, then attach it to the trees on either side. And while another group hides away under the cover of those bushes over there … when they're given the signal to show themselves, they come out of hiding and scare the birds into taking flight. Good timing is vital to the exercise, for just as the birds start flapping their wings to take to the air, the hunters send their boomerangs whizzing above their heads to try to fool them into thinking they're in danger of being swooped down upon by birds of prey.'

He was hanging on my every word. 'And as the birds try to fly above the surface of the water … just low enough to keep out of harm's way, some of them fly into the net and become entangled.'

'Ingenious,' he muttered: 'Quite ingenious.'

He was eager to see more before it got too dark, but with a storm approaching and daylight fading, I suggested we put up our tents and camp for the night.

The rain had been holding off as we sat around the fire, and he turned to me and said: 'It's been quite a day William. This land is beautiful beyond belief. It seems that you escaped from hell only to discover your own paradise,' then he reached for his field book and began occupying himself with the rest of his notes.

It seemed that he'd had enough of talking for the moment, so I took the opportunity of bidding him goodnight before settling in for an early night.

We were hoping to cover some twenty-odd miles when we set off at sunrise the following morning, and as we began passing through a field of bracken a short time later, I paused for a moment and broke a piece off:

'The Wathaurong call this *moolaa*. It doesn't taste the best but if you boil up its leaves, you can drink it like tea for the relief of aches and pains.'

I bent down and pulled out a piece by the roots:

'And this sap from its roots can be used to help ease the sting of insect bites.'

He watched me crush up a piece in the palm of my hand:

'If you ever get stung by a wasp or a bull ant, just rub some of this sticky stuff on and it will help to ease the pain.' A part of me enjoyed the fact that he seemed to take an interest in everything he saw, so I pointed to the tree we were standing beside: 'Touch this bark. It feels like paper doesn't it? The tribes use strips of it to wrap around a fractured arm or a leg.'

'Tell me more William. I want to learn as much as you are able to teach me,' so I offered to take him to a village that I knew of, and an hour or so later we were standing there among a group of native huts:

'There's no one living here at the moment but they will be back in the springtime when times of plenty come around again.' I went across to one of them and looked inside: 'I once stayed here with my family years ago.'

'Your *family?*'

'Yes, my Wathaurong family,' and I told him of the slaying and the place where I had buried them. 'How horrible William. When did it happen?'

'Many years ago. Not long after I'd escaped from the settlement.'

'How far is it from here to where the killings took place?'

'A couple of hours or so.'

I had a pretty strong feeling what was about to come next, and he wasted no time in confirming my suspicions: 'How would you feel about taking us there?'

The day was descending into lengthening shadows by the time we arrived at the gorge that leads upriver to where the waterfall spills down the rock face. And as he gazed all around him trying to take it all in, I pointed out the hollow tree I had slept in on most of the occasions that I'd come here.

'Do you mind if we stop for a while? I would like to do a sketch of the place.'

While he was busy doing so, I had wandered off on my own and soon found myself at the bend in the river where Trawalla and I had laid our traps, and a whole lifetime of memories came flooding back over me. I sat down on a log and began reflecting upon where life had taken me... with all the twists and turns that it throws our way, and I'd been off in a world of my own for God knows how long, when the sound of Mister Wedge's voice drew me back in:

'There you are William. I was worried that you might have abandoned us.'

From Dreamtime to Armageddon

A short time later a little further upriver, we were standing by the gravesite when I turned to him and said: 'I come here every spring to look after them.'

It seemed as if he was seeing me for the very first time:

'That's wonderful William. It's very touching.'

I did not know which way to look, so I looked up at the sky:

'It will be dark soon. I suggest we make camp for the night.'

We were sitting around the fire later when the sun had gone down, when he looked in my direction and his gaze met mine: 'It's a hauntingly beautiful place William,' before going on to say: 'Did I tell you that I've been giving names to landmarks during my travels … to rivers and mountains and significant things that I felt were of importance?'

'I knew you were taking notes and drawing sketches, but I didn't know you were giving things names.'

'Yes. I've been doing so since the very first day I arrived,' and as he opened his field book to show me what he'd written, I felt compelled to say:

'My eyes are not what they used to be. Can you read it to me?'

'Of course William,' as he pointed to the page:

'See this sketch?' I nodded my head while admiring his handiwork.

'I have written underneath the drawing what I have decided to call this beautiful place. I have given it the name of Buckley's Falls.'

I could not find the words with which to respond, so I sat there in silence while he in turn went back to working on his notes.

We had been travelling for most of the following morning when we happened upon some Wathaurong people whom I had not seen for months, and we were ever so glad to meet up again.

Delighted to have been given the opportunity to spend time with the locals, Wedge wrote in his diary later that night:

"We fell in with two families of natives who were very friendly. Nullamboin (with whom Buckley had lived had never seen a white man before. He had heard of a gun and the effects of it and was anxious to see me let it off. On my preparing to do so he evinced great fear, and requested that I go further off. Buckley told him that I would not hurt him or anyone – He then sat down and was grateful at my hitting a small piece of paper set up as a mark – The two families were bivouacked about fifty yards from each other and I pitched my tent between them. The whole party of natives (11) remained sitting around my fire till about 10 o'clock, when I intimated I wished to go to bed & they instantly retired to their own quarters. They kept up a conversation a great part of the night among themselves and with Buckley – they were anxious to know where I had been and why I was walking about the country. Mon 24th of August - After breakfast I took leave of the natives. Nullamboin and his wife were sorry at Buckley's leaving them and shed tears on our starting."

Wedge would later write a report entitled:

"Narrative of an Excursion Amongst the Natives of Port Phillip,"

where he described them as follows:

"They are astonishingly dextrous in the use of weapons employed by them in the defence of their persons, and in procuring food; and in tracking each other, as well as the kangaroo, and other animals they are very expert.

From Dreamtime to Armageddon

JHW: 'Buckley Falls, 20 August, - a normally minor rapid below which the upper Barwon, presumed aboriginal 'Worrigong' by Wedge, turns northward from eastward, and within half a mile blends with the Moorabool river, when both veer southward as Wedge's aboriginal Barwon, variously spelt.

The most trifling disarrangement of the grass, a broken twig or the slightest thing which indicates the direction of the object of pursuit is at once perceived by them. They follow the track with ease at a brisk pace – on several occasions I witnessed their adroitness in this respect. In fact their perceptions in seeing, hearing and smelling are surprisingly acute – and in the pursuit of their game, they evince that patient perseverance so peculiar to man living in a state of nature."

He had been reading it to me as he wrote it all down, and I had been warming to him more and more with every passing day. He had a childlike fascination for everything and everyone that he came into contact with, and his genuine concern for all of God's creatures made it a genuine pleasure to spend time in his company. So much so that it had been a week or so of carefree joy, but when we finally returned to Indented Head at the end of our travels, we found more of the Wathaurong had arrived there while we'd been away. They had heard that strange white men had settled there and had begun giving out food and all manner of gifts. But as there was now a shortage of supplies and too many mouths to feed, I was given the task of trying to explain the state of affairs.

To make matters worse, now that I was back to wearing white man's clothes, there were some among them who had already begun to regard me with a degree of suspicion. Here was I … at sixes and sevens as to which side of the fence on which I belonged … seen as little more than oddity to a handful of whites, and a traitor to some of the Wathaurong who had previously regarded me as a part of the family. But I was determined to make do in spite of all that, and had been helping with the tasks that required extra hands, when several days later Mister Wedge informed us that he was going on an excursion to Mister Batman's land at the top of the bay, and advised me to remain here just in case there was trouble.

While Wedge was away he wrote:

"Near the northern extremity of the Port, two rivers form a junction and their united waters are discharged into the Port together. Both these rivers are navigable for vessels of about sixty tons, for five or six miles above the junction.

The country between these rivers extending to the north forty or fifty miles, and to the east about twenty five miles, to a tier of mountains which range from the back of Western Port. The soil is a sandy loam and is generally of good quality, and in some of the valleys very rich: the surface is everywhere thickly covered with grass. I think very highly of this part of the country and consider it to be well adapted for agricultural pursuits. It will be desirable to form townships at the head of the salt water in each of these rivers. The river coming from the eastward is called by the natives **Yarra-Yarra.** *Here and there along the shore of the Port, and along the course of the river, the plains are quite open, as much so as the heaths of Cambridgeshire. I have no doubt they will become valuable sheep stations for breeding flocks. There is a great deficiency of timber fit for building and fencing purposes, the want of which will be seriously felt in this part of the country, whenever it becomes thickly inhabited. On the whole, I think favourably of the country for the general purposes of colonization."*

Upon their arrival up at the river, Wedge found some of John Pascoe Fawkner's people were already there, and were preparing the ground to start farming there on Batman's land, and as they refused to budge when he asked them to do so, Wedge wrote to inform Batman in Van Diemen's Land. Meanwhile, Batman had taken the request for Buckley's pardon directly to Governor Arthur and when he had got the answer he was hoping to hear, he wasted no time in writing to Wedge:

"I have only time to say two words, the Governor told me half an hour ago that he would give Buckley his pardon, and get it confirmed – this is all right – they are all pleased on this side. I hope your Account will accord with mine – as respects the land it has done so. Will forward said pardon along with any other relevant correspondence aboard the very next vessel that is coming your way."

That vessel was the Henty family's cutter *Mary Ann,* and it arrived at Port Phillip on 13th of September. You could have heard Buckley cheering for miles around when he was given the news. And although Wedge happily took part in the celebrations, he had other concerns that required his attention.

Meanwhile, several weeks earlier in New South Wales, Governor Bourke had issued a proclamation voiding Batman's treaty in the name of the Crown …

while, unaware that bigger things were being played out behind the scenes, Wedge was worried that they might be in danger of losing their Port Phillip holdings to a group of interlopers, so he and Henry Batman decided to leave a few men at Indented Head to look after their land, and took Buckley along with them to relocate themselves to the *Yarra Yarra*.

I was up on deck gazing out to sea when Mister Wedge came over and stood beside me: 'It's a beautiful night William.'

'I think spring is on the way,' came my reply.

And as a wave broke over the bow he turned to me to say:

'You must have had more than your share of difficult times over these past thirty years.'

'Yes, you could say that I've had my moments.'

'Do you have family William … back home in England?'

'I have two sisters and a brother, but I haven't seen them in nearly fifty years.'

As I paused to reflect, I added: 'My mother and father sent me away to live with my grandparents when I was six years old,' adding as I thought more about it:

'Times were hard and they were finding it a struggle to feed us.'

Another wave hit the bow and the spray took to the air on gossamer wings.

'How did it feel to be sent away like that?'

Finding an answer did not come easy:

'I suppose I got used to it after a while.'

Now it was he that gazed out to sea:

'I intend to return to Van Diemen's Land soon so I can sell my land there. My plan is to come back here and settle down.' He paused for a moment as his gaze met mine: 'I was thinking … now that you are a free man again, would you like me to speak to the appropriate authorities while I'm down there and request a grant of land for you up here at Port Phillip?'

Once again my response took its time in coming:

'There was a time in my life when I would not have thought that I'd reach the age of forty. Yet here am I now, at the tail-end of my fifties with no possessions or family to speak of. Even if I *did* have a house and a piece of land ... with no sons and no daughters to bequeath it to, I wouldn't know what to do with it.'

Now it was *he* who took his time in responding:

'William ... I am confident that a person with your depth of experience in dealing with the natives could find plenty of opportunities for employment here. You could carve out a future for yourself if you were of a mind to do so.'

I dwelled for a moment upon what he had said:

'To be honest ... I've been at sixes and sevens since coming here. It's as if I'd found myself but now I'm lost again, and I'm not really sure that is what I'm looking for.' He reached out and touched my arm:

'It may take time, but I'm sure you will find yourself again. Give some thought to what I've said,' adding as gazed off into the moonlight:

'But don't take too long William. When opportunity knocks you cannot afford to be sitting idly on your hands.'

Silence came between us, until he turned to me to say:

'The world is changing William. We need to change with it or we'll be left behind,' before adding: 'When I visited the Yarra Yarra recently, I found there were already other settlers there farming the land that Mister Batman had purchased from the natives.'

I could not prevent myself rising to the challenge:

'Do you really believe that the land belongs to you and your associates?'

He became defensive all of a sudden:

'I know how you feel about the natives William, but we have their best interests at heart too. That's why I would not like to see anyone undermine the good work we are trying to achieve. Our aim is not only to reimburse them but to teach them Christian values and lead them down the path to civilisation.'

Although we were standing together side by side ... I doubt that we could have been any further apart, and it saddened my heart to have heard him say it. Silence came to settle, only this time it stood like a wall between us.

It seemed he'd said all there was to say, for he yawned and stretched then bid me goodnight before heading off down below decks.

They arrived at the Yarra Yarra on the following day and found the settlers Wedge had referred to were already working the land and planting their crops.

It goes without saying that Batman and Wedge were most annoyed at seeing them there, but being determined as they were to avoid jeopardising their holdings by stirring up trouble, they chose instead to let sleeping dogs lie.

And after unloading their supplies and pitching their tents, they began concentrating their efforts on settling in.

By the time Wedge sailed for Van Diemen's Land a few days later, Buckley and Henry were hard at work building a hut for Batman's family.

As the days passed by, more and more natives had begun to arrive in the hope of receiving food and supplies. Some were from the Bunurong tribe, who reside on the peninsula where Governor Collins had tried to establish the settlement at Sullivan Bay, while the others were Wurundjeri people, who inhabit the region around the settlement. Because both of these tribes had a history of feuding with the Wathaurong clans ... and as Buckley was known to have an allegiance with the Wathaurong people, there were many among them who suspected his motives. The other concern for Buckley was that that these tribes spoke different dialects than the Wathaurong people, so communication was anything but easy.

Things didn't get any better for him when John Pascoe Fawkner arrived a few weeks later. Like Batman, Falkner was the son of a convict, but *unlike* Batman ... he was a bad-tempered vindictive fellow who seemed to live by the principle that if you couldn't find something derogatory to say about someone, then you might as well say nothing at all. And because he regarded anyone who had an affiliation with Batman and the Port Phillip Association as being part of the enemy camp, he took an instant dislike to Buckley and never missed an opportunity to cast malicious and spurious accusations against him whenever he could.

By now, word was out that the Crown had revoked Batman's treaty and that they intended to sell off the land to all and sundry.

Meanwhile, in the hope of being given preferential treatment for the money they had spent on gifts for the natives, members of the Association were still moving full speed ahead, as was the case when John Batman arrived at Port Phillip on 9th of November with a cargo of 500 sheep, forty casks of pork and three or four tons of flour and other food supplies. Henry had asked Buckley to call in the natives in anticipation of his brother's arrival, and hundreds arrived to welcome him.

The event was recalled decades later by William Barak, who would live until 1903, and be the last full-blood tribal leader of the Wurundjeri people ... the traditional owners of Melbourne and the Yarra Valley.

Barak wrote in his short memoir ... *'My Words:'*

"I was about eleven years old when Batman visited Port Phillip Bay. I never forgot it ... all the blacks camp at Muddy Creek. Next morning they all went to see Batman, old man and women and children, and they all went to Batman's house for rations, and killed some sheep by Batman's order. Buckley told the blacks to look at Batman's face. He looks very white. Any man that you see out in the bush not to touch him. When you see an empty hut not to touch the bread in it. Make a camp outside and wait till the man come home and finds everything safe in the house. If you kill one white man, white fellow will shoot you down like a kangaroo."

As much as Batman had been looking forward to coming back to stay, his failing health prevented him from remaining too long, and as his primary goal was to sell his land in Launceston and bring his family back over to settle, he set sail again for Van Diemen's Land as soon as he was able.

Following that visit, Batman had written:

'Here I cannot refrain expressing my thankfulness to that good Providence which threw Buckley our way, for certainly he has been the medium of successfully establishing between us and the natives an understanding which, without his assistance, could never have been effected to the extent it has been.

It leaves no room to doubt the most beneficial results in proof of the most favourable state of intercourse with them."

The next Association member to set sail for Port Phillip was Joseph Gellibrand, and he boarded the *Norval* on 17th of January with his sixteen year old son Tom. The ship was carrying a cargo of sheep belonging to Captain Swanston, and having been pounded by a howling gale on the trip across the strait ... as the vessel was ill-equipped for carrying livestock in stormy conditions, more than a hundred sheep perished during the voyage. And when the storm prevented them from entering *The Heads*, they were forced to put ashore in Westernport Bay.

The following is an extract of what Gellibrand later wrote:

"When the sheep were landed they endeavoured to drink salt water, and were inclined to wander (as sheep always do in a strange place). They were put ashore upon a point of land with abundance of grass, and 300 acres of land might be enclosed by a line of 150 yards. When I landed, I particularly cautioned the shepherds not to let the sheep stray, and to keep them from salt water.

We then proceeded to examine the land and found abundance of grass, and in some places it was six feet high; but we did not find any water."

With the full force of the summer sun blazing down upon them, Gellibrand left the shepherds with most of what was left of their water supply, while he and the others set off to walk to the Yarra Yarra settlement in search of help. Gellibrand's group were found two days later by a group of natives and brought to the settlement … all blistered and burnt and suffering from heat stroke.

Seeing the settlement for the very first time … Gellibrand wrote the following when the group had recovered:

"The settlement consists of about a dozen huts, built with turf on the left bank of the river Yarra Yarra. The river, from the mouth to the settlement, is about eight miles long; it is salt for about six. The first two miles, it is about 500 yards wide; for the next three miles, it is about 300 yards.

It then becomes gradually narrower, and is about 60 yards wide at the settlement, with deep and precipitous banks. Vessels of 60 tons burthen can with safety proceed to the settlement, close to the shore and discharge their cargo. I made arrangements with Mr. Batman to despatch, on the next morning, four Sydney natives who were quite confident that they would be able to find the sheep, and bring them back to Port Phillip."

The following day on the 1st of February, he added more to his notes:

"I had, this morning, a long conversation with Buckley, and explained to him very fully the desire of the Association, in every respect, to meet his views, and to make him superintendent over the native tribes, for the purpose of protecting them from aggressions, and also of acting as an interpreter in imparting to them not only the habits of civilization, but also of communicating religious knowledge.

Buckley appears to be of a nervous and irritable disposition, and a little thing will annoy him much, but this may arise from the peculiar situation in which he has been placed for so many years. I am quite satisfied that he can only be acted upon by kindness and conciliation, and that by those means he will be an instrument in the hands of Providence in working a great moral change upon the aborigines. He is not at all desirous of occupying any land or having sheep, but is highly pleased at the idea of being appointed superintendent of the natives, with a fixed stipend. I told him that I intended on the following day to proceed to Geelong, and inquired whether he would not like to visit his own country. He seemed very much pleased at the idea, but stated he did not think he could walk so far. I then proposed he should ride, which seemed to gratify him very much, and in consequence I engaged a large cart-horse of Mr Fawkner's for that purpose."

After setting off again the following day, he wrote:

"We reached Indented Head about four o'clock, and I learned, to my extreme mortification, that some of the natives had that morning quitted the settlement, in consequence of the threats made by the man at the station that he would shoot them.

I found that the natives had a few nights previously stolen about a sack of potatoes out of the garden; they had pulled up the roots and taken the potatoes, and then planted the roots in the earth again. I found, in answer to my inquiries, that no food of any description had been given to the natives for the last three months."

His notes read as follows the following day:

"We started very early this morning, under the expectation that we should see the natives, and in order that they should not be frightened, I directed Buckley to advance, and we would follow him at a distance of a quarter of a mile. Buckley made towards a native well, and after he had ridden about eight miles we heard a cooey, and when we arrived at the spot, I witnessed one of the most pleasing and affecting sights. There were three men, five women, and about twelve children. Buckley had dismounted, and they were all clinging round him, and tears of joy and delight running down their cheeks. It was truly an affecting sight, and proved the affection which these people entertained for Buckley. Among the number were a little old man, and an old woman, one of his wives. Buckley told me this was his old friend, with whom he had lived and associated for thirty years. We gave them a few presents, and then left them to proceed on our journey."

While the next day's entry stated:

"We started this morning about six o'clock, and continued our course until we reached the junction of the Yalloak and Barwon Rivers and went across to a spot called Buckley's Falls, where there is a large basin, and the river somewhat resembles the cataract and basin at Launceston, but upon a smaller scale.

Buckley showed us the hollow tree in which he used to live and the places where the natives used to catch fish in the winter season."

After being out exploring for nearly two weeks, when they got back to the Yarra Yarra, Gellibrand wrote:

"Upon my arrival back at the settlement I found about 150 natives, and I learnt with much concern that an act of aggression had been committed upon one of the women, which required my immediate attention. Without waiting to refresh myself or refit, I proceeded to the native huts, and ordered the person supposed to be implicated to be brought down. I found a young woman, about 22. This woman had been proceeding toward the settlement to see her mother, and fell in with one of the shepherds, who laid hold of her, brought her to his hut, tied her hands behind her, and kept her there all night and abused her person. When she reached the settlement she communicated to her friends the injury she had sustained, and they immediately apprised Buckley of it, expecting to obtain redress. The natives – men women and children – assembled around me. I explained to them, through Buckley, our determination, in every instance to punish the white man, and to protect the natives to the utmost of our power. I directed that the man be immediately sent for, and if the woman identified him as the aggressor, that he should be removed from the settlement by the first ship, and be publicly taken away as a prisoner, and they were highly satisfied."

After that, Gellibrand booked passage on the *Caledonia* so he could go back to Van Diemen's Land and attend to his business. He was busy ... they were *all* busy, as what some might refer to as the wheels of progress slowly gained momentum. Wedge had sold his land in Van Diemen's Land and returned to Port Phillip to establish his station on the Werribee River ... the settlement on the Yarra Yarra was steadily expanding as every new vessel brought an influx of pioneers eager for land ... while back in Van Diemen's Land, John Batman's health had improved sufficiently for him to be able to finally relocate himself over to Port Phillip.

And on the 20th of April, the *Caledonia* sailed up the Yarra Yarra, bringing Batman, his wife and their seven daughters along with Miss Caroline Newcomb ... the girls' governess. He'd barely had time to step ashore, when he was greeted with the news that clashes between the settlers and the natives were becoming more frequent. And with the Sydney authorities determined to maintain control ... the following month, the *New South Wales Government Gazette* formally proclaimed that the Aborigines of Port Phillip were under the Governor's protection, stating:

"Whereas it has been represented to me that a flagrant outrage has been committed upon the Aboriginal Natives of Western Port by a party of white men, and that other outrages of a similar nature have been committed by stockmen and others upon the Natives in the neighbourhood of Port Phillip; Now, therefore I, the Governor ... do hereby proclaim ... that the whole of the country on the southern coast of New Holland extending westward from Wilson's Promontory to the 129th degree of East Longitude ... being within the limits of New South Wales, all persons residing or being within the same, are subject to the Laws in force in the said Colony, and the promptest measures will be taken by me to cause all persons who may be guilty of any outrage against the Aboriginal Natives, or any breach of the said Laws to be brought to trial before the Supreme Court of New South Wales, and punished accordingly."

Wedge also recorded an incident where some of the Bunurong tribe had been shot by men who were stripping wattle bark on the Mornington Peninsula, with his findings reading as follows:

"Buckley had despatched messengers to request that the wounded natives might be brought to this place and on the 11th instant (March) the families arrived, and on visiting their huts I found that four individuals had received gunshot wounds. It appears that the natives were fired upon soon after sunrise whilst lying in their huts, and one young girl about thirteen years of age was wounded in both her thighs (by a ball passing through both legs). The girl's mother, when rescuing her daughter, was fired on and wounded in the arm and the shoulder."

In another incident, two of Captain Swanston's shepherds had been killed by Wathaurong tribesmen near Indented Head, and an old Aboriginal man had described the event to one of Batman's employees, who reported what he'd been told as follows:

"The men were on their way with a pack-bullock laden with provisions for the Werribee Station, and were met by a tribe near the Murradock Hill. They were both armed with fowling pieces, which caused the wary tribe to entrap them by stratagem, thus:

By persuading one that he could shoot an emu, they got him to accompany a portion of their party to one side of the hill, whilst under the pretence of having shot a kangaroo, they prevailed upon the other to go in a contrary direction, and the separated men were attacked and killed."

In another instance, a settler by the name of Charles Franks had been killed along with one of his shepherds and their supplies had been stolen. After their bodies had been discovered, a party of armed settlers led by Henry Batman set out in search of the perpetrators. Fawkner assembled a party of his *own,* and whilst in the process of doing so … pointed the finger of blame at Buckley for inciting the natives to violence. *His* party met up with Henry Batman's group the following day, and they followed the natives' tracks for the next three days, before they finally caught up and took them by surprise.

When news of the occurrence had spread all the way down to Van Diemen's Land, the *Cornwall Chronicle* printed the following account of what had then taken place:

"We learn that a party of settlers assisted by the Sydney natives connected with Mister Batman's establishment, and a few domesticated natives of the settlement, started in quest of the murderers, whom they were fortunate enough to fall in with at no great distance from where the bloody deeds were perpetrated. We have no positive assurance of their number, but learn that it was considerable, and that many of them were clothed in the articles of dress plundered from their victims. A quantity of provisions and other stores were likewise in their possession, which left no doubt as to their identity. The avenging party fell upon the guilty tribe about daylight in the morning, having watched them the previous night, and putting into effect a pre-concerted plan of attack, succeeded in annihilating them – This tribe, which we now presume to be no longer troublesome, were it appears, a particularly treacherous people – less numerous than any of the others, and despised by all."

As various accounts of what had occurred began filtering through to the authorities in Sydney, Governor Bourke appointed thirty six year old Captain William Lonsdale to the role of Port Phillip magistrate, and he arrived in HMS *Rattlesnake* on 29th of September accompanied by his wife and his children and three constables. Although this was to be the official beginning of colonial rule in Port Phillip ... it would seem Lonsdale was less than impressed with the settlers there, and wrote in his diary a short time later:

"Although emigrants from Van Diemen's Land are constantly arriving, scarcely any of them are persons of respectability, or would be considered desirable members of any community."

Lonsdale's regiment was the King's Own Regiment of Foot ... Buckley's old regiment from years before, and he employed the former convict as a constable and interpreter at a salary of sixty pounds a year including rations.

Buckley's duties were to include going out into the countryside to visit the settlers, to try to promote a sense of confidence between them and the natives, and though things seemed to have settled down for a while, before too long Lonsdale began to receive reports of more violent incidents occurring ... for in much the same way as what had occurred in Sydney Cove and Van Diemen's Land, there were ever-increasing numbers of whites now occupying traditional Aboriginal hunting grounds, determined to go to any lengths to hang onto their new found gain. And with no soldiers on hand to protect them, many had no hesitation in resorting to violence at the end of a gun.

It was mainly left to Buckley and Batman's Sydney natives to try to maintain friendly relations between both parties. That was until the 5th of October, when the *Stirlingshire* arrived from Sydney bringing thirty more soldiers and the same number of convicts. In addition to the men it brought, the brig also carried a supply of timber and bricks, along with more blankets and supplies to keep the Aborigines satisfied. It also brought news that Governor Bourke wanted a census of the settlement carried out. This was commenced on the 27th of October 1836, and recorded the following details:

There were 44 land owners ... although the one's who'd claimed the lion's share for themselves ... three of which were Wedge, Charles Swanston and Joseph Gellibrand ... were absentee landowners still residing in Van Diemen's Land. Their stock at Port Phillip included 41,332 sheep, 155 head of cattle and 75 horses, whilst a mere 97 acres of land were under cultivation.

Several months after the census was completed, word arrived from Sydney that Governor Bourke *himself* planned to visit Port Phillip, and when the news reached Joseph Gellibrand down in Van Diemen's Land, he decided to go there and meet the Governor to find out first-hand what plans the Crown had in mind for the fledgling colony. Gellibrand planned to travel there with his son Tom, and a man by the name of George Hesse ... a barrister friend from Van Diemen's Land, and they arrived at Indented Head aboard the brig *Henry* on the 21st of February.

Upon their arrival, they discovered that the Governor was not expected for perhaps another week, so Gellibrand decided to spend that time inspecting the countryside. His plan was to ride to the station of Captain Swanston before going on to the Yarra Yarra settlement, where he hoped to arrive within three or four days. The men were able to hire two horses from a settler named Thomson, but as he was unable to spare a third, it was decided that Gellibrand's son Tom would remain with the *Henry*, then re-join the others up at the settlement.

The Governor however got there first ... arriving at the Yarra Yarra on the 4th of March with his entourage of fifteen. Getting right down to business, Bourke had the government surveyor Robert Hoddle draw up a grid for the proposed layout of the town, and after appointing Buckley as his interpreter and guide, he had him muster some hundred or so natives so they could be paraded before the official party, where they were given blankets and clothing as well as official instructions on how they were expected to behave in a white man's world. Expressing a desire to see more of the interior ... he then engaged Buckley to lead their party on a tour of the countryside, and this is how Buckley later described it:

"We crossed the Yawang Plains and reached the Marrabul (now called the Esk River) on the first night, there pitching our tents.

The night following we halted near the Yallock where we again bivouacked, remaining there several days; His Excellency, the Surveyor-General and others, taking me with them and moving in various directions expressing great delight at what they saw of the country in that quarter. The natives we met with in these excursions were, through me, assured by the Governor that if they came to the settlement and avoided committing any offences against the white people, they should receive presents of all kinds of useful articles. These invitations and promises many of them availed themselves of, behaving very peaceably. About this time we received intelligence that Mister Gellibrand had again arrived from Hobart Town, in company with a Mister Hesse, a solicitor of that city. It appeared that shortly after arriving at Geelong, they had left that place on horseback for the settlement, but at the end of a fortnight, great alarm was excited by news that they had not arrived at the latter – nor found their way back to the former."

The brig *Henry* had arrived at the Yarra Yarra while the Governor's party were out exploring, and when Gellibrand's son found that his father had not turned up as he was meant to have done … a search party was dispatched at once.

Two months later, the *Launceston Advertiser* printed an article on what was reported to have happened next:

"The following account is from a gentleman who came up from Port Phillip in the **Lowestoft** … the last vessel to arrive from the settlement; the latter is communicated by a gentleman who received his information by letter from a resident at Port Phillip by the same vessel:

'The distressing absence of Mr. Gellibrand and Mr. Hesse caused me, when at Port Phillip, to travel from the settlement to Geelong, in order to obtain the most authentic information of everything connected with their fate. As I am aware how deeply interesting the subject is now felt by the public, I am induced to place before them all the information that I could collect from two gentlemen (Mr. Cowie and Mr. Stead) who went in search of Messrs. Gellibrand and Hesse after their absence had caused so much apprehension. The last station at which Messrs. Gellibrand and Hesse slept was at Captain Pollock's.

On leaving there they proceeded, accompanied by a man named Aiker as a guide, for the purpose of reaching a station of Captain Swanston's situated upon the River Leigh, as it was supposed Aikers knew where to ford the river. The junction of two rivers, the Byron and the Leigh is the place near where the ford was thought to be, and that junction was no more than nine miles from Captain Pollock's. They travelled the entire day after crossing the river, without coming to the station Captain Swanston. Aiker states that during the course of the day's journey, he mentioned to Mr. Gellibrand he was sure they were going the wrong way, but Mr. Gellibrand was of a contrary opinion. The following morning Aiker declined going any further in that direction, and determined upon returning back to Captain Pollock's where he arrived the middle of the following day."

The *Launceston Advertiser* also reported the incident:

"They started from Captain Pollock's and took with them the man Aiker to conduct them to the spot where he had parted from Messrs. Gellibrand and Hesse; the whole of the party were mounted, and travelled about thirty five miles the first day, and arrived in the place where the missing gentlemen had parted with Aiker. In travelling this route, the party found that instead of crossing the Leigh river, Messrs. Gellibrand and Hesse, together with Aiker crossed the Byron. They slept upon the bank, thinking it to be the Barwon- which circumstances no doubt was the first cause of their losing their way. The party in search proceeding from this spot, traced the marks of Mr. Gellibrand's and Mr. Hesse's horses about six miles further up the banks of the river, where they crossed about four miles of plain into a thick wood; here they continued to follow the marks of the horses for about six miles further, when all traces were lost. These tracts were in a westerly direction and in the opposite course to the settlement. The party travelled the wood for an entire day in various directions, and returned, after an absence of eight days, without making any further discovery."

Now that word the was out concerning their disappearance, Buckley had been recalled from the Governor's excursion to enable him to take part in a *second* search party, and he gave this account later of what had taken place:

"I was sent on horseback in search of them; and upon reaching the hut of a man nearly fifty miles distant, I remained there to wait for Mr. Gellibrand's son.

They had taken with them as a guide a white man, who, according to his statement, they had discharged in consequence of some misunderstanding about the direction of the route. I engaged some trustworthy natives and accompanied them, hoping to trace the steps of the horses. After necessary refreshment, we traced the spoor of the horses, as the Cape men say, much farther on, into an extensive plain recently burnt, and here we lost it altogether. We now struck across country; and falling in with a native encampment, and having reason to think it was not a tribe likely to receive the white men in a friendly manner, I requested them to remain where they were whilst I endeavoured to obtain some information. After I had approached them and dismounted and they had all come round me in a friendly manner, just as I began explaining the object of my visit, our white party rode up, and by this interference prevented me doing my service. The abrupt appearance of our people on horseback, so much alarmed the natives that I could do nothing *except to offer that I be permitted to accompany them alone to their camp as they wished, but this my companions would not allow me to do, not feeling safe in my absence. Our efforts to trace the lost travellers were all in vain, and at length I returned to the settlement to report our ineffectual efforts for their rescue."*

Being on a tight schedule, Governor Bourke was unable to wait for the search parties to return, so he performed his last vice-regal duty before departing the colony, that of conferring the name of Melbourne upon the new town ... in honour of Lord Melbourne, the British Prime Minister of the day.

Now with Gellibrand gone ... the Van Diemen's Land banker Captain Swanston became the biggest landowner in the new colony, with his holdings taking up most of what became known as the Bellarine Peninsula. And with increasing numbers of settlers arriving at Port Phillip with every new ship that sailed through *The Heads*, more and more tracts of land were being opened up to meet the increased demand for pastoral pursuits.

To make matters worse for the original inhabitants, after Surveyor-General Thomas Mitchell's journey of discovery ... his party had left a road clearly-marked by wagon wheels for others to follow. This highway to the south became known as the 'Major's Line,' and the conflict with the natives that had occurred along the way, had Mitchell notify London:

"I fear a considerable number of these unhappy savages were slaughtered."

The opening up of this new frontier led to an explosion of the European population, as numbers in Port Phillip increased from approximately 1,000 in 1837, to 20,000 within the next five years. The natives were being dispossessed of a territory that was as big as England, and when they finally began to realise that they were facing the total destruction of their way of life, they started fighting back with a vengeance. With violent attacks on the increase, the squatters wrote to Governor Bourke in Sydney requesting protection, and as a result ... Captain Foster Fyans of the 4th Regiment was appointed as Geelong police magistrate with a staff of two constables, a clerk, and a working party of twelve convict labourers. Fyans' instructions from the Colonial Secretary in relation to his appointment had read as follows:

"From motives of humanity, justice, and true policy, it is most desirable that an amicable intercourse with the native tribes should be cultivated by every possible means from the earliest moment of the occupation of their country, and to this most important object I am directed to call your particular attention ... to facilitate communications with the Aborigines, you will be provided with a competent interpreter ... William Buckley, and I conclude this subject by conveying his Excellency's commands that you report to me by every favourable opportunity your proceedings with regard to the native blacks, and that you consider their protection and welfare to be the primary object of your appointment."

Buckley was witnessing the decline of the Aboriginal way of life from the native perspective and was becoming more and more disillusioned with any form of officialdom. This was evident from Fyans' report following their first meeting:

'I awaited the pleasure of Buckley, who was appointed by the Governor to act and assist the natives about Geelong, under my jurisdiction. I stared when I saw the monster of as man. He was six feet seven inches high, and had resided with the blacks for thirty three years ... 'Now for the road, Mr. Buckley. Have you no blanket?' 'Nothing,' he replied. 'Well take charge of this,' giving him a piece of pork and a good slice of a large damper. 'What!' he said, looking down on me, 'Carry damper and pork! I don't care for such things. I can feed myself; you may do as you like.'

After setting off the following morning, Fyans' party reached their destination later that day... the company station hut on the Barwon River, where they were met by the man who'd been left in charge during the overseer's absence ... a Mr. Taylor. He showed Fyans the instructions the overseer had been given, by producing a letter from the company head in Van Diemen's Land:

"You are neither to allow a black nor a white man to intrude on the property ... pointing out a line where he had received instructions to place a line of fencing from the river to the sea – embracing an extent of ground fearful even to imagine.

I suppose some three or four hundred thousand acres of ground, embracing the entire of the Indented Head."

Although Buckley remained silent ... he could not believe what he was hearing. Governor Bourke had instructed Fyans to assemble and count as many of the Aborigines as possible and to give them blankets, flour and tea as well as distributing two dozen tomahawks. In all, 275 men women and children were counted, but when the goods were given out, there weren't enough blankets for everybody. Then when Fyans had his men throw the tomahawks into the river, all hell was about to break loose. Fyans reacted as follows:

"Fearing bad results from all my visitors, from their general demeanour and manner, and becoming somewhat apprehensive, I ordered my two constables to load and my ten convicts to fall in close to my hut. The natives saw this preparation, and I kept some distance from them with my double barrel gun, accompanied by Mr. Patrick McKeever, the district constable, also armed.

It had the effect of making the natives retire, the interpreter Buckley telling them to do so. After this, I never permitted more than a few to approach the place."

Time would prove Taylor to be a murdering brute, with a hatred for the natives that was second to none. And as Fyans got to learn more about his reputation, he wrote this report the following year:

"Mr Taylor was concerned in the most inhuman murder of a native, who was tied to a tree and shot by one of his men within twenty yards of his door, in the front of his house. The murderer was tried in Sydney and acquitted: why? Because Mr Taylor absconded to Van Diemen's Land until the trial was over, when he and the fellow that committed the most wilful murder returned, and were retained in their employ at Indented Head. I suppose for the purpose of preventing any Native from visiting the place, which was the chief part of the country for their hunting and fishing, and in fact their great support."

Government minutes read as follows two years later:

"The Attorney General should be made acquainted with the fact of the man Taylor's reappearance again at Port Phillip – and acquaint the Law Officers of the fact that in November 1839, the Reverend Benjamin Hurst reported at second-hand a massacre of twenty five natives ... and the name of Taylor was mentioned as connected with it."

Eight months later, George Augustus Robinson (Protector of Aboriginals) wrote this to his superiors:

"Taylor was overseer of a sheep station in the Western District, and was notorious for killing natives. No legal evidence could be obtained against this nefarious individual. The last transaction in which he was concerned was of so atrocious a nature that he thought fit to abscond."

By the following year, Lonsdale's report to Sydney confirmed the fact that relations with the natives were continuing to deteriorate:

"The excitement among the settlers has been general and with much reason as the depredations of the blacks have been numerous, and their attacks can seldom be guarded against ... Mr James Smith's, Mr George Smith's and Mr. Simpson's stations have been attacked besides those I have already reported."

Worse was still to come, and in another incident ... the squatter John G. Robertson recalled:

"The first day I went over to the Wando Vale Station to look at the ground. I found old Maggie (that Sir Thomas Mitchell gave the tomahawk to) fishing for muscles with her toes in a waterhole up to her middle, near where the Major crossed the stream ... nearly all her male relatives were killed three days before I arrived by the Whyte brothers. Three days after the Whytes arrived, the natives of this creek, with some others, made up a plan to rob the newcomers ... they watched for an opportunity, and cut off fifty sheep from the Whyte brothers' flocks, which were soon missed ... they had taken shelter in an open plain with a long clump of tea- tree, which the Whyte brothers' party, seven un number, surrounded and shot them all but one. Fifty one were killed, and the bones of the men and sheep lay mingled together bleaching in the sun at the Fighting Hills ... the females were mostly chased by the men up the Glenelg, and the children followed them."

Another settler by the name of William Moodie was told an even more graphic version of the event by an old Aboriginal man:

"Blackfellow all runem along scrub in creek, lubra lookup scrub, whitefellow shoot her down. Two hundred fine fat lubra shot."

Buckley didn't last long working for Fyans. He could see the writing on the wall and wanting no further part in what he was seeing ... he resigned from his position a short time later.

Another Christmas was just around the corner ... it would be his last in the colony, for he set sail for Van Diemen's Land on the 28th of December 1837 ... never to return to land of the Wathaurong. [9]

---

[9] **Footnotes:**
For a while, Buckley was employed as a gate-keeper at the Female Factory (as it was called) which employed convict women at the Cascades, South Hobart. Then two years later ... he married a young widow named Julia Eggers. After meeting a retired journalist and publisher by the name of John Morgan, they collaborated on the project of writing Buckley's story ... completing the task in 1852. Finally, after a long and eventful life, at the age of seventy six William Buckley was killed when he fell from a cart in which he was travelling.

Severely stricken with illness and on the verge of financial ruin ... John Batman's marriage broke down in 1839, and he died at home at the age of thirty eight. His body was buried in the Old Melbourne Cemetery ... now the site of the present-day Victoria Market. The house in which he spent his last days on Batman Hill was demolished years ago, having stood on the site of what is now part of Southern Cross Railway Station.

I left the last word to Derremart ... an Aboriginal elder from the Bunurong tribe, who fought in vain for the rights of his people to remain on their land on the Mordialloc Reserve.
During his tragic decline, he was recorded as saying:
"You see ... all this mine, all along here Derrimut's once; Why me have lubra? Why me have piccaninny? You have all this place, no good have children, no good have lubra. Me tumble down and die very soon now."

SOURCES

- The Aboriginal Australians: The First Pioneers ... C.H. Berndt and R.M. Berndt.
- Thirty Years Among the Blacks of Australia: The Life and Adventures of William Buckley the Runaway Convict ... William T. Pyke.
- Life and Adventures of William Buckley ... John Morgan.
- Buckley's Hope... Craig Robertson.
- The Land of the Kulin (Discovering the Lost Landscape of the First People Port Phillip) ... Gary Presland.
- The First Residents of Melbourne's Western Region ... Gary Presland.
- The Peninsula Story ... Nepean Historical Society.
- John Pascoe Fawkner's Sullivan Bay Reminiscences ... Edited with notations by Richard Cotter.
- No Place for a Colony... Richard Cotter.
- Voices from Sorrento. The Sorrento Settlement ... Richard Cotter.
- Convicts Unbound. The Story of the Calcutta and their Settlement in Australia ... Marjorie Tipping.

- Aboriginal Australians ... Richard Broome.
- Pemulwuy, the Rainbow Warrior ... Eric Willmot.
- Australia's Aboriginal Heritage ... Jean A. Ellis.
- Macquarie Atlas of Indigenous Australia... Bill Arthur and Francis Morphy.
- The Fatal Shore ... Robert Hughes.
- Land Musters, Stock Returns and Lists, Van Diemen's Land 1803-1822 ... Irene Schaffer.
- Van Diemen's Land ... James Boyce.
- 1835 – The Founding of Melbourne and the conquest of Australia ... James Boyce.
- A History of Tasmania ... Lloyd Robson.
- Forgotten War ... Henry Reynolds.
- David Collins. A Colonial Life ... John Currey.
- Notes on the Sealing Industry of Early Australia ... J. C. H. Gill
- An Account of the Whaling and Sealing Industries of Van Diemen's Land ... L. C. Murray.
- Michael Howe. The Last and the Worst of the Bushrangers of Van Diemen's Land... Thomas E. Wells.
- The Bushrangers. Illustrating the Early Days of Van Diemen's Land ... James Bonwick.
- John Batman. The founder of Victoria ... James Bonwick.
- John Batman. The First Biography This Century ... C. P. Billot.
- John Batman and the Aborigines ... Alastair H. Campbell.
- Sea Wolves and Bandits... L. Norman.
- History of Australian Bushrangers... George Boxall.
- The Companion to Tasmanian History... University of Tasmania.
- The Black War. Fear, Sex and Resistance in Tasmania ... Nicholas Clements.
- Aboriginal Society in North West Tasmania: Dispossession and Genocide ... Ian McFarlane.
- Wathaurong, the People Who Said No ... Bruce Pascoe.
- Black Robinson. Protector of Aborigines ... Vivienne Rae-Ellis.
- Australian dictionary of Biography... Australian National University
- Aboriginal Victorians. A History since 1800 ... Richard Broome.
- Letters from Victorian Pioneers ... T. F. Bride editor.

- The Todd Journal … Published by the Library Council of Victoria.
- On the Country Around Port Phillip … J. H. Wedge Esq.
- John Batman's Rebecca Journal.
- Memoirs recorded at Geelong, Victoria, Australia by Captain Foster Fyans.

… … … …

ABOUT THE AUTHOR

Having worked for the past 15 years as an addictions counsellor, Phillip now devotes much of his time to his love of writing, and lives with his wife Helen in the small seaside town of Mount Martha, 80 kilometres south east of Melbourne.

Printed in Australia
AUOW01n1746080818
301218AU00001B/2